©The Scottish Milk Marketing Board 1992
Underwood Road, Paisley, Scotland PA3 1TJ
Telephone 041-887 1234
ISBN 0 903438 10 0

The Scottish Milk Marketing Board would like to thank
The Stockwell China Bazaar, 67 Glassford Street, Glasgow, G1 1UB
also at 52 George Street, Edinburgh EH2 2LE
for lending china and accessories for use in the photographs.

Design: Alan Wright Design
Photography: Graham Lees
Printed by Harper Collins

by

ELIZABETH MACINTOSH
HOME ECONOMICS MANAGER
SCOTTISH MILK MARKETING BOARD

assisted by
CAROLYN FRASER
and
ALISON SAMPSON

Carolyn Fraser, Elizabeth MacIntosh and Alison Sampson in the studio
during food photography for Milk Magic.

INTRODUCTION

We live in a fast changing world and even something as basic as food has gone through great change in cooking methods, content, way of taking meals and types of food available.

Food should sustain us and be nourishing – it should be an enjoyable experience and for busy people, it shouldn't take too long to prepare.

With these thoughts in mind, the Scottish Milk Marketing Board has published this cookery book. It has up to the minute information on dairy produce, a wide variety of new recipes some of them devised especially for speed of preparation and a step by step section to encourage the new cook to try some interesting dishes. There is a microwave section with recipes which are particularly good when cooked in a microwave oven.

The easy way to tackle the challenge of what to eat to stay healthy is to eat a wide variety of foods and not to eat too much fat, sugar or salt. Don't feel guilty if you indulge yourself occasionally, food should be enjoyed and good food should be treated well, cooked carefully and eaten with pleasure.

Bon appetite!

QUICK RECIPES

This symbol indicates recipes which can be made within 15 minutes.

MILK

Milk remains our one natural food which contains all the nutrients necessary to maintain life and promote body growth.

Because of our less active lifestyles and our greater use of labour saving devices, we don't need foods with so much fat and sugar for energy. With this in mind, the dairy industry has responded to consumer needs and produced a wide variety of milks and dairy products with a low fat content. People can now choose the milk which suits their lifestyle.

THE CARE OF MILK

Milk should be kept cool and covered at all times and kept in a refrigerator.

CHILDREN AND MILK

Young children need a good supply of energy as they are constantly running around. Whole milk is the best milk for them as it not only supplies them with a good amount of calcium, vitamins and minerals but it is also an easily consumed food with a good supply of calories. A government report in 1985 The Committee on Medical Aspects of Food Policy (COMA) – recommended that children below the age of five be given whole cows milk.

There are many ways to encourage children to take milk – in cereals, porridge, hot drinks, soup, rice, milk jelly and puddings. If a child does not like milk to drink on its own, a flavour can be added. This will make a palatable drink which will still give them the nutritional value of milk.

MILK'S CONTRIBUTION IN YOUR DIET

In the 1991 Government COMA Report, reference nutrient intakes became the yardstick by which you could measure your consumption of nutrients.

The table below shows the contribution which a pint of whole milk makes to the daily nutritional requirements of women between the ages of 19 and 50 years.

Percentage contribution which a pint of whole milk makes to the reference nutrient intake (R.N.I.) of energy, protein, fat vitamins and minerals for a woman between the ages of 19 and 50 years.

PERCENTAGE %	5	10	15	20	25	30	35	40	45	50	55	60	65	70	75	80	85	90	95	100
Energy																				
Protein																				
Fat																				
Vitamin A																				
Thiamin																				
Riboflavin																				
Nicotinic Acid																				
Vitamin B6																				
Folic Acid																				
Vitamin B12																				→ 153%
Pantothenic Acid																				
Biotin																				→ 111%
Vitamin C																				
Vitamin E																				
Calcium																				
Iodine																				
Iron																				
Magnesium																				
Phosphorus																				
Potassium																				
Selenium																				
Zinc																				

◆ 20% of a nutrient from a food is a 'useful' source.　　△ 50% of a nutrient is a 'rich' source.

For semi-skimmed and skimmed milk the main changes are in the fat and fat soluble vitamins.

	Fat	Vit A	Vit E	
Semi-skimmed	13%	23%	6%	of R.N.I.
Skimmed	0.8%	1%	trace	

You will see at a glance that a pint of milk is an excellent source of a wide variety of nutrients.

As a rough guide, provision of 20% of the RNI for a nutrient can be taken to mean that the food is a good source of that nutrient. If 50% is provided, the food can be considered a rich source.

For further nutritional information on dairy produce write to the Home Economics Department, The Scottish Milk Marketing Board, Underwood Road, Paisley PA3 1TJ.

The Scottish Milk Marketing Board thank the National Dairy Council for assisting with this information

TYPES OF MILK

Whole Milk – Containing less than 3.9% fat, whole milk is a very popular variety in Scotland and is available everywhere.

Semi-Skimmed Milk – This is milk which has had approximately half the fat removed giving a fat content of 1.5%-1.8%. Like whole milk, semi-skimmed is also popular and widely available in Scotland.

Skimmed Milk – This milk has had almost all the fat removed to produce a product which has a fat content of less than 0.3%.

Homogenised Milk – This is pasteurised milk which by means of forcing the milk through a very fine aperture, breaks down the fat globules and disperses them evenly through the milk.

Channel Islands Milk – Channel Islands milk must contain 4% butterfat and comes from Jersey or Guernsey cattle. It is not retailed widely in Scotland.

Sterilised Milk – Homogenised milk is filled into bottles which are capped with a metal cap and then the milk is heated to a temperature of not less than 100°C (212°F). There is little demand for this milk in Scotland.

U.H.T. Milk – The ultra heat treatment or 'Long Life' as it is sometimes called, is the process of heating homogenised milk to no less than 132°C (270°F) for at least one second and then it is cooled quickly and packaged in foil lined containers. It will keep for at least three months without refrigeration and is ideal for camping, sailing and as a reserve for your store cupboard.

Buttermilk – This is skimmed milk which has been pasteurised and then a special bacteria is added giving the buttermilk its distinctive taste.

FRESH DAIRY CREAM

Some things don't change and the image of cream as a super, top quality accompaniment for either a savoury or a sweet dish still makes people's mouths water. One of the simplest and most popular of sweets is strawberries and cream. Many firms have tried to copy cream but no one has quite captured the flavour or texture of real fresh dairy cream.

There are recipes in the following pages using fresh cream, all quite delicious, for both savoury dishes and sweets.

TYPES OF CREAM ARE DEFINED BY THE PERCENTAGE OF BUTTERFAT IN THEM AND THE LEGAL REQUIREMENTS ARE AS FOLLOWS:

Half Cream	12%
Single Cream	18%
Whipping Cream	35%
Double Cream	48%
Clotted Cream	55%

USES OF CREAM

HALF CREAM – This is a thin pouring cream which is used for coffee or for pouring over sweets or cereals.

SINGLE CREAM – Single cream is homogenised to prevent separation and it may be pasteurised. It can be used for pouring and may be added to sauces. It will not whip.

WHIPPING CREAM – As the name suggests this cream will whip and can be used for filling cakes and piping cream on trifles and cakes. It can also be used in sauces, for pouring and for making ice cream.

DOUBLE CREAM – Double cream can be used in the same ways as whipping and pouring cream. It has a high fat content and this means it will whip more quickly and form a denser cream than whipping and will retain its shape longer after being used for piping or decoration.

SOURED CREAM – This is a single cream which has a culture added to it to give a piquant flavour and a thick texture. It can be used for sweet or savoury dishes. If you want to make your own soured cream, add a teaspoon of lemon juice to a 140ml (¼ pint) carton of single cream.

CREME FRAICHE – This product is made from cream and can be used in any recipe using soured cream. It is ideal for cheesecakes.

FROMAGE FRAIS – This product is made from whole or skimmed milk and is sold as medium fat (8%) or low fat (<1%). It looks and tastes like Greek-style yogurt and is available as plain or fruit flavoured. It can be used in sweet or savoury dishes in the same way as yogurt.

LONG LIFE CREAM – This cream also called Ultra Heat Treated (U.H.T.) cream, comes in three types, single, whipping and double and can be used in place of its fresh counterpart. The cream is heat treated to enable it to be kept not necessarily under refrigeration for up to twelve weeks.

U.H.T. – Milk and cream are handy to have in your cupboard in an emergency should you run short of the fresh product at any time.

STORAGE OF FRESH CREAM

Fresh cream should be kept in its original container. It should be kept cool, preferably in a refrigerator and covered and kept away from strong flavours.

HOW TO WHIP CREAM FOR BEST RESULTS

The cream, bowl and whisk should be really cold. Whip the cream quickly at first with a fork, balloon whisk or rotary whisk and when it begins to thicken and take on a matt finish, beat more slowly until it stands in peaks. An electric mixer is not recommended as it is difficult not to overbeat the cream.

SCOTTISH CHEESE

Scottish cheese has a well earned excellent reputation for flavour and quality. We have also a good variety to choose from and this is being added to each year.

The most popular cheese in Scotland is Scottish cheddar which is used in cooking, in salads, in sandwiches and with biscuits. It is a hard cheese matured for between 4 and 9 months and can be bought pre-packed or in a piece. It is manufactured as red or white cheddar, the difference being that to the red a harmless vegetable dye has been added. This gives the cheese a better colour for cooking. Some people seem to think that white cheese is stronger than red, or vice versa but the strength of the cheese depends on the length of time it has been matured and not on the colour.

There are many recipes to which a little cheese added gives the dish extra flavour and extra nutrients. A supply of grated cheese is a very handy food to have in the fridge for biscuits, sandwiches, sauces or for topping savoury dishes.

A very pleasant way of finishing off a meal is with a cheese board. The range of soft cheese is extensive and ingredients such as oatmeal, nuts, whisky and pepper blend with cheese to give unique flavours.

Remember to have the cheese out of the fridge for a good hour before serving to bring out their full flavours.

Y O G U R T

A food which has absolutely "taken off" in recent years in this country
is yogurt. It has found a place in most peoples diet and is said to aid
longevity. It is one of our most convenient of foods and is often eaten
from the carton from which it comes.

Natural yogurt is a very versatile product which can be used in savoury
and sweet dishes. It adds a unique flavour to savoury sauces which is very
pleasant.

The varieties and flavours are many as are the types. the fat content can
vary and most cartons will give information on the nutritional value of its
contents.

BUTTER

The natural flavour of butter, which is made from pure fresh cream has yet to be equalled in flavour. Nothing can touch the combination of corn on the cob with butter gently melting on it. It is quite delicious.

FREEZING OF DAIRY PRODUCE

The best way to use dairy produce is in a fresh state but if you wish to store some for a while, here are some tips in deep freezing them.

MILK – Homogenised milk can be frozen for up to one month in a plastic container – never freeze liquid in a glass container. If you have too much of other kinds of milk, make into a sauce or sweet and freeze.

CREAM – Single cream does not freeze well but whipping or double cream will freeze best if you whip it lightly and add a little sugar. If you have cream left over pipe the excess onto a metal tray, freeze the rosettes then store in a plastic box.

CHEESE – Cheddar cheese retains a good flavour after freezing although it tends to crumble after it is thawed. Cheese can be grated before freezing and used as required. Soft cheeses tend to become stronger in flavour after freezing.

CONTENTS

The recipes are suitable whether you use skimmed, semi-skimmed or whole milk, you can make the choice. If you are watching your fat intake, you can use low fat cheddar cheese for sauces and dips.

Tomato and Crab Bisque

1 x 300g (10½oz) can condensed
cream of tomato soup

1 soup can fish stock or water

1 x 170g (6oz) can crab meat

2 tablespoons dry sherry

1 teaspoon mixed herbs

2 tablespoons cooked rice or peas

140ml (¼ pint) double cream

Serves 4

METHOD

1. Empty contents of the can into a large
saucepan, gradually add the stock or water.
2. Add crab meat, sherry, herbs, rice or peas
and heat gently until almost boiling. Season.
3. Serve with a swirl of cream.

Prawn & Melon Cocktail

1 x 125g (5oz) carton soured cream

2 tablespoons mayonnaise

2 tablespoons tomato ketchup

seasoning

} Sauce

100g (4oz) prawns

½ honeydew melon

½ lettuce, shredded

paprika pepper

4 lemon wedges

Serves 4

METHOD

1. Blend cream, mayonnaise and tomato
ketchup together. Season.
2. Remove seeds from melon and make
melon balls using a ball scoop (or melon
can be cubed).
3. Place shredded lettuce in the base of
4 glasses.
4. Divide prawns and melon between glasses.
5. Pour sauce over top and sprinkle with
paprika pepper.
6. Serve with buttered brown bread and
lemon wedges.

Peach Marie Rose

1. Put some shredded lettuce on 4 side plates.
2. Divide 50g (2oz) prawns and place in
centre cavity of 4 peach halves. Place peach
halves, rounded side up on the lettuce.
3. Make up sauce as recipe above and spoon
over peach halves.
4. Sprinkle with paprika pepper and serve
with buttered brown bread.

Carrot and Courgette Soup

50g (2oz) butter

1 onion, chopped

225g (8oz) carrots, chopped

225g (8oz) courgettes, chopped

40g (1½oz) plain wholemeal flour

420ml (¾ pint) chicken stock

420ml (¾ pint) milk

seasoning

pinch nutmeg

75g (3oz) cheddar cheese, grated

Serves 6

METHOD

1. Melt butter in pan, add onion, carrots and
courgettes then cover and cook for 5 minutes
over a low heat until soft.
2. Add flour then gradually blend in the stock
and milk.
3. Season and add nutmeg then bring to the
boil and simmer for 20 minutes.
4. Liquidise soup and serve hot sprinkled with
grated cheese.
*NOTE: For a creamier soup, omit cheese and finish
with a swirl of cream.*

Tasty Tomato Soup

25g (1oz) butter

1 onion, chopped

1 x 400g (14oz) can of tomatoes, chopped

2 tablespoons tomato puree

2 slices smoked bacon, chopped

420ml (¾ pint) chicken stock

140ml (¼ pint) milk

50g (2oz) rice, cooked

seasoning

Serves 4

METHOD

1. Melt butter in a large pan and fry onion
and bacon until soft.
2. Add chopped tomatoes, puree, stock, milk
and bring to boil.
3. Allow to simmer for 5 minutes on a low
heat.
4. Add the rice, season and heat through.

Stuffed Mushrooms

6 large flat mushrooms
40g (1½oz) butter
1 small onion, finely chopped
2 rashers bacon, chopped
1 clove garlic crushed (optional)
25g (1oz) wholemeal flour
140ml (¼pint) milk
50g (2oz) cheddar cheese, grated
1 teaspoon mixed herbs
salt and black pepper

Topping

50g (2oz) wholemeal breadcrumbs
25g (1oz) cheddar cheese, grated

Oven temperature: 200°C/400°F/No. 6
Position in oven: centre
Time in oven: 20-25 minutes

Serves 6

METHOD
1. Wipe mushrooms then remove and chop stalks finely. Place in an ovenproof dish.
2. Melt butter in a pan, add onion, bacon, garlic and mushroom stalks and cook for 2-3 minutes.
3. Blend in flour and cook for 1 minute then gradually add milk and bring to the boil, stirring all the time. Cook for 2-3 minutes.
4. Stir in the cheese, herbs and seasoning.
5. Fill mushroom centres with sauce mixture then sprinkle with topping and bake.

Loch Fyne Kipper Paté

225g (8oz) kippers, flaked
50g (2oz) butter
50g (2oz) cream cheese
seasoning
To Serve – Hot buttered toast or oatcakes.

Serves 4

METHOD
1. Combine all ingredients in a food processor or beat until smooth.
2. Season to taste.
3. Spoon paté into a suitable dish and serve with buttered toast or oatcakes.

Spicy Ginger and Corn Soup

50g (2oz) butter

1 teaspoon ground ginger

1 red pepper, finely chopped

1 onion, finely chopped

1 x 340g (12oz) can sweetcorn

560ml (1 pint) chicken stock

50ml (2fl.oz.) milk

50ml (2fl.oz.) single cream

seasoning

Serves 4

METHOD

1. In a large pan melt butter.

2. Add ginger, pepper, onion and cook over a low heat for 3 minutes.

3. Add the sweetcorn and cook for 1 minute.

4. Pour in stock and bring mixture to boil, cover and simmer for a further 5 minutes.

5. Add milk and cream.

6. Rub through sieve (or liquidiser) and return to pan.

7. Season and reheat.

Asparagus Soup

1 x 275g(10oz) can asparagus spears, drained

560ml(1 pint) milk

280ml (½ pint) chicken stock

150g (6oz) cottage cheese

4 sticks celery, roughly chopped

1 tablespoon lemon juice

seasoning

Serves 4

METHOD

1. Place all the ingredients in a blender. Blend at a high speed until smooth and creamy.

2. Pour into a saucepan and heat gently.

3. Adjust seasoning and serve.

Creamy Barley Broth

*50g (2oz) pearl barley, washed and soaked
overnight in 280ml (½ pint) water*

25g (1oz) butter

1 carrot, chopped

½ turnip (225g/8oz), chopped

1 onion, chopped

2 sticks celery, sliced

1 small leek, sliced

840ml (1½ pints) chicken stock

280ml (½ pint) milk

70ml (⅛ pint) single cream

seasoning

Serves 4-6

METHOD
1. Melt butter in pan, add prepared
vegetables, cover pan and sauté gently
without browning for about 5 minutes,
stirring occasionally.
2. Add barley and water and stock to pan,
then bring to the boil, cover and simmer for
about 1 hour, until barley is soft.
3. Stir in milk and cream. Season.
4. Serve garnished with chopped parsley.

Summer Avocado Soup

2 ripe avocados

2 tablespoons lemon juice

420ml (¾ pint) milk

140ml (¼ pint) single cream

salt and pepper

Serves 4

METHOD
1. Remove the stones and skin from the
avocados and chop the flesh.
2. Blend the avocado, lemon juice, milk and
cream in a blender until smooth.
3. Season to taste.
4. Chill well before serving garnished with
chives.

Garlic Bread

1 Vienna loaf, sliced

75g (3oz) butter, softened

2 cloves garlic, crushed

Oven Temperature: 200°C/400°F/No.6
Position in oven: top
Time in oven: 10 minutes

Serves 6-8

METHOD
1. Mix butter and garlic well.
2. Spread mixture on each slice of bread and
place on a baking sheet.
3. Place in oven for 10 minutes.
This gives lovely golden crunchy garlic bread.

German Vegetable Soup

25g (1oz) butter

3 rashers back bacon, chopped coarsely

1 x 300g (10½oz) can condensed lentil soup

1 x 300g (10½oz) can condensed vegetable soup

2 soup cans milk

100g (4oz) cocktail sausages, cut into small slices

150g (6oz) packet mixed vegetables

Serves 6

METHOD
1. Fry bacon rashers gently in a large
saucepan, stir in the contents of both cans
and gradually add the milk.
2. Add sausages, vegetables and stir until
almost boiling. Simmer gently for 5 minutes.

Smoked Salmon Cornettes

100g (4oz) smoked salmon

100g (4oz) cottage cheese

100g (4oz) tuna fish (drained)

seasoning

Serves 4

METHOD
1. Divide salmon into eight portions.
2. Mix tuna fish, cottage cheese and season.
3. Place a spoonful of mixture onto the pieces
of salmon and roll up into a cornette.
4. Serve two each on a plate with a little salad
and lemon.

Country Style Paté

225g (8oz) chicken livers, washed and chopped
225g (8oz) lean bacon, chopped
1 small onion, chopped
1 clove garlic, crushed (optional)
150g (6oz) fresh white breadcrumbs
1 teaspoon mixed herbs
seasoning
2 eggs
140ml (¼ pint) milk

Oven temperature: 170°C/325°F/No. 3
Position in oven: centre
Time in oven: 1 hour

Serves 8

Farmhouse Lentil Soup

1 carrot, chopped
1 onion, chopped
¼ turnip, diced
1 large potato, diced
50g (2oz) butter
100g (4oz) lentils
2 tablespoons fresh parsley, chopped
560ml (1 pint) milk
280ml (½ pint) chicken stock
seasoning
140ml (¼ pint) single cream

Serves 4-6

METHOD
1. Mix together in a bowl the chicken livers, bacon, onion and garlic then stir in the breadcrumbs, herbs and seasoning.
2. Beat the eggs and milk together and add to mixture.
3. Liquidise until smooth and place in a 1kg (2lb) buttered loaf tin. Cover with foil and bake in oven.
4. Cool in tin then turn out. Serve with hot buttered toast or crusty bread.

METHOD
1. Melt butter in pan and gently fry vegetables for 10 minutes.
2. Add lentils, parsley, milk and stock. Season.
3. Bring to the boil then cover and simmer for 1 hour.
4. Cool slightly, liquidise and stir in cream.

Seafood Paté

1 x 100g (4oz) can red salmon	
1 x 100g (4oz) can tuna fish	
1 x 100g (4oz) can shrimps	
75g (3oz) fresh white breadcrumbs	
50g (2oz) butter, melted	
1 lemon, juice and grated rind	
140ml (¼ pint) single cream	
seasoning	

Serves 8

Cheesy Corn Chowder

25g (1oz) butter	
1 onion, finely chopped	
2 sticks celery, finely chopped	
675g (1½lbs) potatoes, diced	
560ml (1 pint) milk	
420ml (¾ pint) chicken stock	
1 teaspoon thyme	
black pepper	
100g (4oz) gammon steak, cooked and chopped	
1 x 340g (12oz) can sweetcorn and peppers	
150g (6oz) cheddar cheese, grated	

Serves 6

METHOD
1. Drain salmon, remove skin and bone and flake. Drain and flake tuna fish then mix salmon and tuna together in a bowl.
2. Drain shrimps and mash with a fork then add to salmon and tuna.
3. Add breadcrumbs, butter, lemon juice and rind and cream to bowl. Season and beat well.
4. Using an ice cream scoop make 8 portions of paté. Chill well.
5. Transfer each paté portion to a side plate and garnish with salad ingredients.
6. Serve with lemon and hot buttered toast.

METHOD
1. Melt butter in pan, add onion and celery and fry gently until soft.
2. Add potatoes, milk, stock, thyme and seasoning then bring to the boil, cover and simmer for 20 minutes until the potatoes are tender.
3. Add gammon and sweetcorn and simmer for 5 minutes, Check seasoning then divide chowder between 6 ovenproof bowls.
4. Sprinkle liberally with cheese then grill to brown topping. Serve immediately with fresh crusty bread.

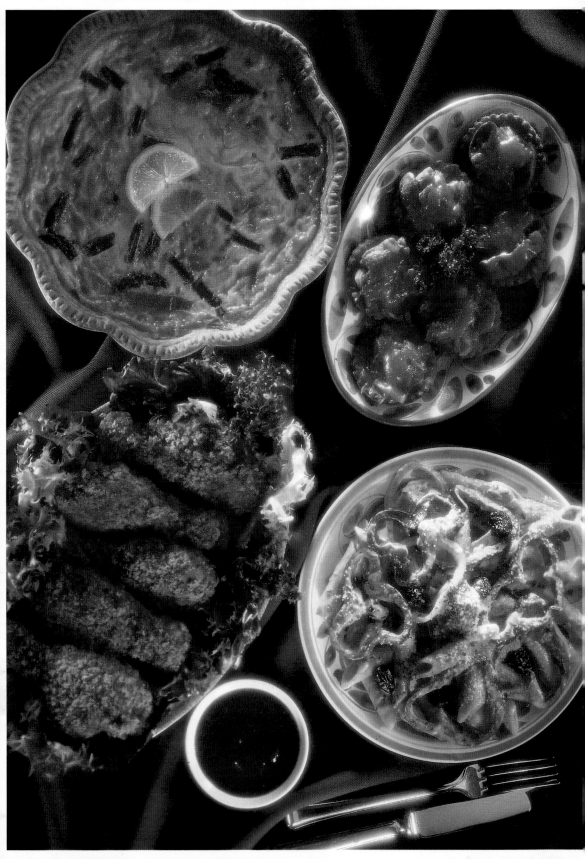

Smoked Salmon and Asparagus Flan

225g (8oz) plain flour, sieved

pinch of salt

100g (4oz) butter, diced

4-5 tablespoons water

280ml (½ pint) milk

2 eggs, beaten

100g (4oz) asparagus, cut into small pieces

50g (2oz) smoked salmon, cut into small pieces

seasoning

Garnish: lemon slices

Oven Temperature: 400°F/200°C/No. 6
Position in Oven: centre
Time in Oven: 30-35 minutes for flan

Serves 6-8

METHOD
1. Put flour, salt and butter into a bowl and rub until mixture resembles fine breadcrumbs.
2. Add water and mix into a dough. Roll out to fit a 23cm (9 inch) flan dish. Prick base and bake blind for 10-15 minutes.
3. Mix milk, eggs, asparagus and salmon together, add seasoning and pour into flan case.
4. Bake until golden brown. Serve hot or cold, garnished with lemon slices.

Golden Chicken Drummers

8 chicken drumsticks

140ml (¼ pint) natural yogurt

2 tablespoons mango chutney

1 teaspoon curry powder

1 tablespoon lemon juice

225g (8oz) brown breadcrumbs

Oven temperature: 200°C/400°F/No. 6
Position in oven: centre
Time in oven: 45-50 minutes

Serves 4

METHOD
1. Remove skin from chicken drumsticks. Mix yogurt, chutney, curry powder and lemon juice together.
2. Dip each drumstick into the yogurt mixture then roll in breadcrumbs.
3. Place on a greased baking tray and bake until chicken is crisp and tender. Turn the chicken over half way through cooking time.
4. Serve with mango chutney.

Crunchy Savoury Tarts

150g (6oz) butter, melted

12 slices white bread, cut into 10cm (4 inch) rounds

1 onion, chopped

100g (4oz) tomatoes, chopped

1 x 125g (5oz) gammon steak, cut into strips

50g (2oz) mushrooms, thinly sliced

1 tablespoon tomato puree

seasoning

100g (4oz) cheddar cheese, grated

Oven temperature: 200°C/400°F/No.6
Position in oven: centre
Time in oven: 23 minutes

Serves 6

METHOD
1. Soak rounds of bread in 125g (5oz) butter and use to line 12 tartlet moulds. Cover with greaseproof paper filled with rice to hold bread in shape while cooking.
2. Bake for 10 minutes, remove paper and rice and bake for a further 10 minutes until crisp.
3. Meanwhile, make the filling. Fry the onions in the remaining butter until golden brown. Add tomatoes, gammon, mushrooms, puree and cook gently for 3-4 minutes. Season.
4. Spoon filling into shells. Sprinkle on the cheese and return to the oven for 2-3 minutes.

Sicilian Pasta

25g (1oz) butter

2 onions, thinly sliced

2 large peppers, thinly sliced

2 tomatoes, chopped

2 cloves garlic, crushed

225g (8oz) penne or other pasta, cooked

50g (2oz) stoned black olives, cut in half

2 tablespoons shredded basil leaves or finely chopped parsley

280ml (½ pint) double cream

parmesan cheese

Serves 4

METHOD
1. Melt the butter in a large saucepan, fry the onions, peppers, over a low heat until soft.
2. Add tomatoes and garlic, cook for a further 2-3 minutes.
3. Add pasta, olives, basil leaves or parsley and seasoning to the vegetable mixture.
4. Stir in the double cream and heat through.
5. Serve immediately with parmesan cheese.

Rosti – Scottish Style

450g (1lb) red wax potatoes (e.g. English Desiree
or Scottish Romano)

25g (1oz) butter

seasoning

1 tablespoon milk

Topping:
2 rashers streaky bacon, cooked and chopped

50g (2oz) cheddar cheese, grated

2 eggs, fried

Serves 2

METHOD
1. Boil the potatoes in skins until semi-tender
the day before.
2. To make Rosti – peel and grate potatoes
using a grater with large holes.
3. Melt the butter in a large frying pan, add
the potatoes and season well with salt and
pepper then using a spatula, press down well.
4. Sprinkle with milk, cover tightly with a lid
and once potatoes are sizzling, reduce heat
and fry gently for 30 minutes to form a brown
crust.
5. Cover the pan with a flat heatproof plate
and flip the potato onto it. Sprinkle with
chopped bacon and grated cheese. Grill to
melt cheese.
6. While Rosti is under grill, fry 2 eggs in a
pan and once cheese has melted, place 2 fried
eggs on top and serve immediately.

Variations:
Bacon Rosti: Finely chop 2 rashers lean bacon
and sauté in the butter before adding
potatoes.

Onion Rosti: Finely chop 1 onion and use in
place of bacon.

Cheese Rosti: Add 50g (2oz) grated cheddar
cheese along with the potatoes.

Baked Potatoes with Savoury Butters

4 baked potatoes (Maris Piper or Cara are best)

slices flavoured butter

Herb 'n' Garlic Butter:
100g (4oz) butter

2 cloves garlic, crushed

2 teaspoons mixed fresh herbs, chopped

Lemon Parsley Butter:
100g (4oz) butter

15g (½oz) fresh parsley, chopped

juice ½ lemon

pinch cayenne pepper

Hot Spicy Butter:
100g (4oz) butter

teaspoon turmeric

teaspoon chilli powder

pinch paprika pepper

Mint Butter:
100g (4oz) butter

4 teaspoons concentrated mint sauce

Serves 4

METHOD
1. Savoury butter should be made in advance
and chilled well. Cream the butter in a bowl
until smooth then blend in the ingredients
and beat well.
2. Shape the butter into an oblong roll, wrap
in greaseproof paper and twist ends then chill
in refrigerator until required.
3. Bake potatoes (Page 33) then remove from
oven, cut a large cross on top of each potato
and squeeze at base to enlarge cut. Serve hot
with slices of flavoured butter.

Cottage Cheese and Pineapple Flan

Cheese pastry

150g (6oz) plain flour, sieved

seasoning and mustard

75g (3oz) butter

25g (1oz) cheddar cheese, grated

Filling

225g (8oz) Cottage cheese

1 teaspoon fresh chives, chopped

seasoning

1 x 425g (15oz) can pineapple slices, drained

2 eggs

140ml (¼ pint) milk

Oven temperature: 170°C/325°F/No. 3
Position in oven: centre
Time in oven: 30 minutes

Serves 4-6

METHOD
1. Sieve flour and seasoning together in a bowl.
2. Rub in butter, then mix in cheese.
3. Bind together with sufficient water to make a stiff dough.
4. Roll out pastry and line a 20cm (8") flan ring and bake 'blind' at 180°C/350°F/No. 4 for 10-15 minutes. Allow to cool.
5. Chop pineapple rings – reserving 4 for garnish.
6. Mix cottage cheese with chopped pineapple and fresh chives. Season.
7. Beat eggs and milk together then blend with cottage cheese mixture.
8. Pour into flan and bake. Serve garnished with pineapple slices.

Tuna Quiche

225g (8oz) plain flour

pinch of salt

100g (4oz) butter, chopped into pieces

4-5 tablespoons cold water

225g (8oz) tuna fish

100g (4oz) cheddar cheese, grated

2 eggs, beaten

5 tablespoons milk

140ml (¼ pint) single cream

seasoning

25g (1oz) cornflakes, crushed

1 tomato, sliced

Oven temperature: 200°C/400°F/No. 6
Position in oven: centre
Time in oven: 40 minutes

Serves 4-6

METHOD
1. Place flour and salt in a large bowl. Add the butter in pieces and rub into the flour until it resembles fine breadcrumbs.
2. Add the water and mix into a dough using a fork.
3. Knead lightly on a floured work top. Roll out pastry to line a 20cm (8") flan dish. Prick base and bake blind for 15 minutes.
4. Fill flan case with tuna fish and cheddar cheese.
5. Beat eggs, milk and cream together, add seasoning and pour mixture into flan.
6. Sprinkle on cornflakes and bake. Garnish with tomato slices.

Cauliflower Quiche

150g (6oz) plain wholemeal flour
50g (2oz) porridge oats
pinch of salt
100g(4oz) butter
340g(12oz) cauliflower, cut into sprigs
3 eggs
70ml (⅛ pint) milk
140ml (¼ pint) single cream
25g(1oz) button mushrooms, thinly sliced
seasoning

Oven Temperature:	190°C/375°F/No. 5
Position in oven:	centre
Time in oven:	40 minutes

Serves 6-8

METHOD
1. To make pastry put flour, oats and salt in a bowl. Rub in butter until the mixture resembles fine breadcrumbs then bind together with enough cold water to give a firm dough.
2. Roll out pastry and line a 23cm (9") flan dish then bake blind at 200°C/400°F/No. 6 for 10-15 minutes.
3. Cook cauliflower sprigs in boiling salted water until just tender. Drain and place in flan case.
4. Whisk together the eggs, milk and cream. Add mushrooms and season. Pour into flan case and bake in oven until lightly set.

Savoury Pitta Pockets

225g (8oz) cottage cheese
100g (4oz) cheddar cheese, grated
2 pineapple rings, chopped
50g (2oz) lean ham, cubed
25g (1oz) raisins
seasoning
4 pitta bread

Serves 4

METHOD
1. Warm pitta bread in oven for 5 minutes then cut in half and open up to make a pocket.
2. In a large bowl, mix together cottage cheese, cheddar cheese, pineapple, ham, raisins and seasoning.
3. Divide mixture between warm pitta pockets and serve as a snack lunch.

Vegetable Chow Mein

225g (8oz) thread egg noodles
50g (2oz) butter
1 green pepper, cut into strips
1 yellow pepper, cut into strips
1 x 225g (8oz) can water chestnuts, sliced
2 cloves garlic, crushed
1 onion, sliced
1 carrot, cut into strips
100g (4oz) mushrooms, sliced
1 teaspoon Chinese seasoning
5 tablespoons soy sauce
100g (4oz) beansprouts
140ml (¼ pint) natural yogurt

Serves 4

METHOD
1. Cook noodles following packet instructions.
2. In a wok or large frying pan, melt butter and fry peppers, water chestnuts, garlic, onion, carrot and mushrooms for 2-3 minutes.
3. Add Chinese seasoning, soy sauce, beansprouts and noodles and heat through.
4. Stir in yogurt and heat gently without boiling, serve immediately.

Speedy Snack

4 slices Vienna loaf, buttered both sides
4 slices gammon
4 slices cheddar cheese
4 pineapple rings
4 teaspoons chutney
dried herbs

Oven temperature:	180°C/350°F/No. 4
Position in oven:	Top
Time in oven:	10 minutes

Serves 4

METHOD
1. Lay bread on a baking tray.
2. Sprinkle a pinch of mixed herbs on top of butter.
3. Place a slice of ham over each piece of bread.
4. Place a pineapple ring on top of each slice of ham, put a spoonful of chutney into the pineapple ring then top with a slice of cheese.
5. Place in oven for 10 minutes and serve immediately.

French Bread Pizza

1 French bread stick, thinly sliced
25g (1oz) butter
1 onion, finely chopped
1 clove garlic, finely chopped
400g (14oz) can chopped tomatoes
2 tablespoons tomato puree
1 teaspoon dried mixed herbs
1 teaspoon sugar
50g (2oz) ham, finely chopped
75g (3oz) cheddar cheese, grated
freshly chopped parsley to garnish

Oven temperature: 200°C/400°F/No. 6
Position in oven: centre
Time in oven: 15 minutes

Serves 4-6

METHOD
1. Toast one side of each slice of bread.
2. Melt the butter, add the onion, garlic and cook until onion softens.
3. Add tomatoes, puree, herbs, sugar and simmer until mixture thickens.
4. Place the bread soft side down onto baking sheets. Spread the tomato mixture onto the toasted side. Bake for 5 minutes.
5. Place the chopped ham on the pizzas and top with cheese. Return to oven for a further 10 minutes.
6. Garnish with parsley.

Lemon Broccoli Pasta

150g (6oz) wholewheat pasta
50g (2oz) butter
50g (2oz) wholemeal flour
560ml (1 pint) milk
100g (4oz) cheddar cheese, grated
seasoning
225g (8oz) broccoli florets
rind and juice ½ lemon
25g (1oz) wholemeal breadcrumbs

Serves 4

METHOD
1. Cook pasta in boiling salted water for 15 minutes. Drain well.
2. Blend the flour with the milk in a saucepan, add the butter and bring to the boil stirring continuously until the sauce thickens and boils. Cook for 1-2 minutes.
3. Remove pan from heat and stir in half the cheese. Season.
4. Cook the broccoli in boiling salted water for 13 minutes or until tender.
5. Drain broccoli and place in the base of a shallow ovenproof dish.
6. Sprinkle lemon rind and juice over broccoli then cover with pasta and cheese sauce. Sprinkle with remaining cheese and breadcrumbs and brown under a hot grill.

Cheddar Chilli Potato Skins

4 medium baking potatoes

25g (1oz) melted butter

seasoning

Chilli Filling

225g (8oz) lean minced beef

1 onion, chopped

1 teaspoon mild chilli powder

1 x 225g (8oz) can chopped tomatoes

1 x 200g (7oz) can red kidney beans, drained

100g (4oz) cheddar cheese, grated

Oven temperature:	200°C/400°F/No. 6
Position in oven:	centre
Time in oven:	1-1¼ hours

Serves 4

METHOD

1. Wash, dry and prick potatoes with a fork then bake in oven until tender. Remove potatoes and turn oven up to 220°C/425°F/No.7.
2. Cut potatoes in half lengthwise and scoop out most of potato being careful not to split the skins.
3. Place potato skins on a lightly buttered baking tray and brush them all over (inside and out) with melted butter. Sprinkle with seasoning and bake for 10 minutes until crisp.
4. To make chilli – brown minced beef in a pan then add onion and chilli powder and cook for 1-2 minutes. Add tomatoes and beans and simmer for 20-30 minutes. Season and stir in cheese.
5. Fill baked potato skins with cheddar chilli filling and serve with a crisp green salad.

Stuffed Peppers

6 green or red peppers

1 x Brown Rice Salad (See page 44)

Oven Temperature:	190°C/375°F/No.5
Position in oven:	centre
Time in oven:	30-40 minutes

Serves 6

METHOD

1. Cut tops off the peppers, remove seeds then stand peppers in a baking dish.
2. Make up brown rice salad and divide equally between peppers. Sprinkle with extra cheese, pour 4 tablespoons of water into the dish, cover with foil and bake until peppers are tender. Serve hot.

Lamb Ratatouille Bake

50g (2oz) butter
1 onion, chopped
1 clove garlic, finely chopped (optional)
225g (8oz) courgettes, chopped
1 medium aubergine (225g/8oz approx), chopped
1 red pepper, chopped
450g (1lb) minced lamb
1 x 400g (14oz) can chopped tomatoes
4 tablespoons red wine
1 teaspoon mixed herbs
salt and freshly ground black pepper
100g (4oz) tagliatelle noodles, cooked and drained
Topping: 1 x 125g (5oz) carton natural yogurt
1 egg
50g (2oz) cheddar cheese, finely grated

Oven Temperature:	190°C/375°F/No. 5
Position in Oven:	centre
Time in Oven:	20-30 minutes

Serves 4-6

METHOD

1. Melt butter in pan, add onion and garlic and fry for 2-3 minutes. Stir in courgettes, aubergine and pepper and cook stirring until soft.
2. Remove vegetables from pan. Place minced lamb in pan and brown well. Drain off any excess fat.
3. Return vegetables to pan and stir in tomatoes, wine, herbs and seasoning. Bring to the boil and simmer for 15-20 minutes.
4. Add cooked noodles to lamb mixture, mix well then place in an ovenproof dish.
5. Beat egg and yogurt together, stir in cheese and spread over the lamb. Bake in oven.

Chicken and Orange Stir Fry

50g (2oz) butter
340g (12oz) chicken breasts, cut in thin strips
100g (4oz) leeks, finely sliced
100g (4oz) courgettes, cut into thin strips
100g (4oz) carrots, cut into thin strips
2 oranges, peeled and segmented
75g (3oz) cashew nuts
70ml (⅛pt) white wine
140ml (¼pt) double cream
salt and pepper

Serves 4

METHOD

1. Melt the butter in a large frying pan or wok and cook the chicken gently for 5-6 minutes, stirring frequently, add seasoning.
2. Add leeks, courgettes and carrots and cook for a further 3 minutes then add wine and heat.
3. Add cream, nuts, seasoning and oranges. Heat through and serve immediately with rice or noodles.

Chicken Filo Parcels

25g (1oz) butter
6 boneless chicken breasts (each 100g/4oz in weight)
1 tablespoon white wine
100g (4oz) smooth cottage cheese
2 spring onions, finely chopped
seasoning
6 sheets filo pastry, thawed
75g (3oz) butter, melted
sesame seeds

Oven temperature:	220°C/425°F/No. 7
Position in oven:	centre
Time in oven:	20-25 minutes

Serves 6

METHOD

1. Melt butter in a pan and brown chicken breasts on both sides then add white wine and sauté gently for 10-15 minutes. Drain and cool.
2. In a bowl mix cheese, spring onions and seasoning together.
3. With a sharp knife, cut a lengthwise pocket in each breast and fill with cheese mixture.
4. Lay a sheet of filo pastry on a chopping board. Brush with melted butter. Place chicken breast stuffing side down at one end of pastry then fold the short edge over chicken and fold again to enclose chicken. Continue to fold chicken in pastry to end of strip and seal edges with melted butter. Tuck the two open ends underneath to make a neat parcel and seal with melted butter.
5. Make 5 more filo parcels and place all 6 on a buttered baking tray. Brush lightly with melted butter and sprinkle with sesame seeds.
6. Bake in oven until crisp and golden. Serve immediately with fresh vegetables.

Crofters Pie

1 x 450g (1lb) haggis	
225g(8oz) mince	cooked and cooled
50g(2oz) mixed vegetables	
450g(1lb) potatoes	
450g(1lb) turnip	
150g(6oz) cheddar cheese, grated	
25g(1oz) butter	
4 tablespoons milk	
seasoning	

Oven temperature: 200°C/400°F/No.6
Position in oven: centre
Time in oven: 15-20 minutes

Serves 4-6

METHOD
1. Mix haggis and cooked mince then place in the base of an ovenproof dish.
2. Peel and chop potatoes and turnip and cook in boiling salted water for 15-20 minutes until tender. Drain well then mash with butter and milk until smooth, season.
3. Mix the cheese with the potato mixture and spread on top of haggis and mince then bake in oven.

Cidered Pork and Apple Stir Fry

50g (2oz) butter
340g (12oz) pork fillet, cut into thin strips
½ teaspoon ground allspice
½ teaspoon cinnamon
1 tablespoon cider
1 eating apple, sliced finely
225g (8oz) packet stir fry vegetables
140ml (¼ pint) soured cream

Serves 4

METHOD
1. Fry pork in butter using a wok or frying pan. Cook gently for 5-6 minutes until tender, stirring continuously.
2. Stir in seasoning and cider.
3. Add apple slices, vegetables and stir fry for a further 4 minutes.
4. Lower heat, add cream and stir well. Serve with rice or noodles.

Chicken Doves with Mint Dressing

4 large chicken breasts, skinned

Stuffing:

25g (1oz) brown breadcrumbs

25g (1oz) no-need-to-soak apricots, chopped

1 teaspoon coriander

1 tablespoon parsley, freshly chopped

2 garlic cloves, peeled and crushed

1 small chilli, finely sliced

25g (1oz) butter, for frying

Dressing:

140ml (¼ pint) double cream

1 x 125g (5oz) carton natural yogurt

*2 tablespoons fresh chopped mint or 1 teaspoon
mint sauce*

Oven Temperature: 220°C/425°F/No.7
Position in Oven: centre
Time in Oven: 30 Minutes

Serves 4

METHOD

1. Place chicken breasts on a chopping board. Using a sharp knife, cut through chicken breast horizontally to make a pocket, make sure you do not cut straight through chicken.
2. Mix the stuffing ingredients together and divide mixture between the chicken breasts, packing the mixture tightly into each pocket and secure with cocktail sticks.
3. Melt butter and fry chicken parcels until golden on both sides. Remove cocktail sticks very carefully.
4. Cut 4 rectangular sheets of foil about 30 x 35 cm (12 x 14 inches).
5. Put each chicken breast on a sheet of foil.
6. Bring the foil up and over the chicken to make a long sausage. Fold top edges together. Twist one end of the foil to make the bird's head and fan the other end into a tail taking care not to tear the foil.
7. Arrange parcels on a baking tray and bake.
8. To make dressing, whip cream and yogurt together until a spooning consistency, stir in the mint.
9. Serve doves on a dinner plate, hot or cold accompanied with dressing and a side salad.

Cheesy Shepherds Pie

25g (1oz) butter
1 onion, finely sliced
1 clove garlic, crushed
450g (1lb) lean minced beef
140ml (¼ pint) beef stock
150g (6oz) packet frozen mixed vegetables
2 tablespoons brown sauce
seasoning
450g (1lb) cooked mashed potatoes
225g (8oz) cheddar cheese, grated
4 tablespoons milk
25g (1oz) butter

Oven temperature: 190°C/375°F/No. 5
Position in oven: centre
Time in oven: 30 minutes

Serves 4

METHOD
1. Fry onion in butter until cooked but not brown, add garlic.
2. Add mince to pan and stir until browned.
3. Add stock and simmer slowly for ½ hour.
4. Remove pan from heat, add mixed vegetables, brown sauce and seasoning to mince, stirring well.
5. Spoon mince mixture into an ovenproof dish.
6. Make topping by mixing potatoes, cheese, milk and butter together. Spoon or pipe the topping over the mince.
7. Place dish in oven and bake.

Whisky Liqueur Steaks

4 fillet steaks, fat removed
1 clove garlic, finely chopped
seasoning
25g (1oz) butter
1 onion, finely chopped
100g (4oz) button mushrooms, sliced
2 teaspoons lemon juice
2 teaspoons Worcester sauce
140ml (¼ pint) double cream
2 tablespoons Drambuie

Serves 4

METHOD
1. Rub steaks with garlic and seasoning.
2. Melt butter in a large frying pan, fry steaks on each side until brown, remove to a warm serving dish to keep hot.
3. Fry onions and mushrooms in the pan until tender. Add lemon juice and Worcester sauce and bring to boil.
4. Stir in cream and Drambuie, lower heat and cook for a further 4-5 minutes or until sauce thickens.
5. Check seasoning and pour sauce over steaks.

Gingered Beef Stir Fry

150g (6oz) pasta spirals
3 tablespoons soy sauce
2 tablespoons rice wine or dry sherry
225g (8oz) rump or fillet steak, cut into thin strips
25g (1oz) butter
1 teaspoon ground ginger
1 teaspoon Chinese seasoning
1 onion, finely chopped
1 green pepper, cut into strips
1 red pepper, cut into strips
50g (2oz) beansprouts
100g (4oz) sweetcorn
2 tablespoons fresh parsley, chopped
140ml (¼ pint) natural yogurt

Serves 4

METHOD
1. Cook the pasta in boiling water, according to packet instructions.
2. Place soy sauce, rice wine or sherry in a bowl, add the beef strips and leave to marinate in the refrigerator overnight.
3. Melt the butter in a large frying pan or wok, cook the beef for 2-3 minutes, stirring continuously.
4. Add the spices, onion, peppers and stir fry for 3-4 minutes.
5. Add the pasta, beansprouts, sweetcorn, parsley and stir gently.
6. Stir in yogurt and heat through without boiling, serve immediately.

Borders Lamb Pie

450g (1lb) minced lamb	
25g (1oz) butter	
1 large onion, chopped	
280ml (½ pint) lamb stock	
1 teaspoon mixed herbs	
seasoning	
225g (8oz) mixed vegetables	
225g (8oz) self raising flour	
25g (1oz)*cornflour	
75g (3oz) shredded beef suet	
280ml (½ pint) milk	

Oven temperature:	180°C/350°F/No. 4
Position in oven:	centre
Time in oven:	30-40 minutes

Serves 4-6

METHOD
1. Melt butter in a large pan and fry onion until soft. Add minced lamb and cook stirring until browned. Drain off excess fat.
2. Add stock, seasoning, herbs and mixed vegetables then simmer for 15-20 minutes. If necessary, thicken juices with 2 teaspoons cornflour, blended with a little water.
3. Meanwhile, place the self raising flour, cornflour and suet in a bowl and gradually blend in the milk to give a thick batter. Season.
4. Place the lamb mixture in a 1.1 litre (2 pint) pie dish. Cover with the batter mixture and bake in oven until risen and golden brown.

Italiano Pasta Bake

225g (8oz) pasta, cooked	
15g (½oz) butter	
450g (1lb) lean minced beef	
1 clove garlic, crushed	
1 teaspoon chilli powder	
1 teaspoon oregano	
salt and freshly ground black pepper	
1 x 225g (8oz) can tomatoes, drained and chopped	
1 tablespoon tomato puree	
225g (8oz) cottage cheese	
140ml (¼ pint) soured cream	

Oven temperature:	180°C/350°F/No. 4
Position in oven:	centre
Time in oven:	20 minutes

Serves 4

METHOD
1. Melt butter in a large frying pan. Turn the heat up and quickly brown the mince for about 2 minutes.
2. Add the crushed garlic, chilli powder, oregano, seasoning and stir in the tomatoes and puree. Lower the heat and continue to cook for a further 10 minutes, stirring occasionally.
3. Blend the cottage cheese and soured cream together.
4. Spoon the pasta into the bottom of a buttered casserole dish and cover with cottage cheese and soured cream mixture.
5. Top with the meat sauce and bake.

Meatballs in a Spicy Sauce

450g (1lb) minced beef

1 teaspoon turmeric

1 teaspoon ground ginger

salt and black pepper

1 small onion, finely chopped

1 egg, beaten

seasoned flour

15g (½oz) butter

425g (15oz) can spicy soup

2 tablespoons tomato puree

2 tablespoons mango chutney

140ml (¼ pint) natural yogurt

Serves 4

METHOD
1. Bind mince, seasoning, onion and egg together. Form the mixture into small balls about the size of a walnut.
2. Roll each ball in seasoned flour.
3. Melt butter in a large saucepan and brown meatballs, stir in soup, puree and chutney.
4. Cook gently for about 25 minutes, turning once during cooking.
5. Before serving, remove pan from the heat and stir in yogurt.
6. Serve on a bed of rice or noodles.

s{L{A}}DS

Crunchy Citrus Salad

2 oranges
1 grapefruit
2 slices bread
25g (1oz) butter
100g (4oz) cheddar cheese, cubed
1 stick celery, chopped
50g (2oz) raisins
2 tablespoons fromage frais
1 teaspoon citrus pepper (or salt and pepper)

Serves 4

METHOD
1. Peel oranges and grapefruit and cut into segments.
2. Remove crusts from bread, cut into 1cm (½") cubes and fry in the butter until croûtons are crisp and golden.
3. Put fromage frais in a bowl and blend in pepper. Fold cheese, celery and raisins into dressing.
4. Reserve one or two segments for garnish and fold remainder into salad.
5. Just before serving, mix through bread croûtons and serve garnished with citrus segments.

Eggs Supreme

9 eggs, hard boiled
280ml (½ pint) double cream
seasoning
225g (8oz) cottage cheese

Serves 8-10

METHOD
1. Whip cream until thick, season.
2. Chop eggs retaining one egg yolk for garnish and add to cream, mix well.
3. Spread mixture in the base of a shallow dish then top with cottage cheese.
4. Garnish with sieved hard boiled egg yolk.

Tuna Twist Salad

150g (6oz) three colour pasta twists, cooked and drained
1 x 100g (4oz) can tuna fish, drained and flaked
100g (4oz) cheddar cheese, cubed
1 x 198g (7oz) can sweetcorn and peppers
¼ cucumber, diced

Dressing:

½ x 125g (5oz) carton soured cream
1 tablespoon milk
1 tablespoon mayonnaise
1 teaspoon chopped fresh mint
seasoning

Serves 4-6

METHOD
1. Blend milk, mayonnaise and soured cream in a bowl to make dressing. Season and stir in fresh mint.
2. Add pasta, tuna fish, cheese, sweetcorn and cucumber. Mix well.
3. Serve in a bowl garnished with a sprig of fresh mint.

Barley Salad

1 x Barley Vegetable Crunch recipe (See page 81)
100g (4oz) cheddar cheese, grated

Serves 6-8

METHOD
1. Cook Barley Vegetable Crunch in microwave oven. Add boiling water in place of stock. Once cooked, stand covered until completely cold.
2. Transfer barley mixture into a bowl. Mix in grated cheese and serve.

Cheddar and Apple Salad

½ iceberg lettuce, washed

140ml (¼ pint) natural yogurt

1 tablespoon mayonnaise

1 teaspoon lemon juice

1 teaspoon caster sugar

225g (8oz) cheddar cheese, cubed

2 dessert apples, peeled, cored and diced

2 canned pineapple rings, coarsely chopped

25g (1oz) sultanas

25g (1oz) mixed nuts

Serves 4-6

METHOD
1. Shred lettuce and use to cover base of a suitable dish.
2. Mix yogurt, mayonnaise, lemon juice and caster sugar together.
3. Fold in remaining ingredients and pile mixture over the lettuce.

Brown Rice Salad

150g (6oz) brown rice, cooked

50g (2oz) button mushrooms, sliced

4 spring onions, sliced

25g (1oz) raisins

1 tablespoon fresh parsley, chopped

50g (2oz) toasted flaked almonds

100g (4oz) cheddar cheese, grated

salt and freshly ground black pepper

Serves 4-6

METHOD
1. In a bowl, mix together sliced mushrooms, spring onions, raisins, parsley, almonds and cheese.
2. Add rice and mix well. Season and serve.

Crisp Green Coleslaw

3 tablespoons milk

3 tablespoons mayonnaise

seasoning

225g (8oz) white cabbage, shredded

½ green pepper, cut into thin strips

¼ cucumber, cut into thin sticks

2 sticks celery, finely chopped

50g (2oz) white cheddar cheese, grated

Serves 4-6

METHOD
1. Blend milk and mayonnaise in a bowl to make a dressing. Season.
2. Add shredded cabbage, green pepper, cucumber, celery and cheese and toss in dressing.
3. Transfer to a salad bowl and serve.

Party Coleslaw

140ml (¼ pint) natural yogurt

1 tablespoon vinegar

1 teaspoon caster sugar

½ teaspoon salt

½ teaspoon French mustard

225g (8oz) white cabbage, shredded

2 tablespoons red pepper, chopped

1 red apple, peeled, cored and diced

100g (4oz) cubed pineapple, canned or fresh

1 carrot, grated

To Serve: lettuce leaves or fresh pineapple halves

Serves 4-6

METHOD
1. Combine yogurt, vinegar, sugar, salt and mustard. Mix thoroughly.
2. Mix cabbage, red pepper, apple, pineapple and carrot together. Add dressing and toss lightly.
3. Arrange coleslaw on a bed of lettuce or use to fill fresh pineapple halves.

Prawn & Corn Puff

Choux Pastry:

50g (2oz) butter
140ml (¼ pint) milk
65g (2½ oz) plain flour, sieved
2 eggs, beaten
100g (4oz) cheddar cheese, grated
seasoning

Filling:

25g (1oz) butter
25g (1oz) plain wholemeal flour
1 tablespoon dry sherry
140ml (¼ pint) milk
140ml (¼ pint) double cream
seasoning
100g (4oz) prawns
100g (4oz) sweetcorn

To Garnish: paprika pepper

Oven temperature: 200°C/400°F/No. 6
Position in oven: centre
Time in oven: 25-30 minutes

Serves 4

METHOD

Choux pastry:

1. Place butter and milk in pan and bring to boil. Remove pan from heat and quickly beat in the flour until mixture is smooth then gradually add eggs, beating well until mixture is smooth and shiny and stands in soft peaks. Stir in cheese and seasoning.

2. Pipe mixture (1cm/½") plain pipe or spoon around edges of a buttered ovenproof dish and bake in oven.

Filling:

3. Melt butter, stir in flour, sherry, milk and cream then heat, stirring constantly until sauce thickens. Season. Add prawns and sweetcorn and heat through.

4. Fill centre of choux ring with sauce and serve immediately sprinkled with paprika.

This is an ideal starter if cooked in individual gratin dishes.

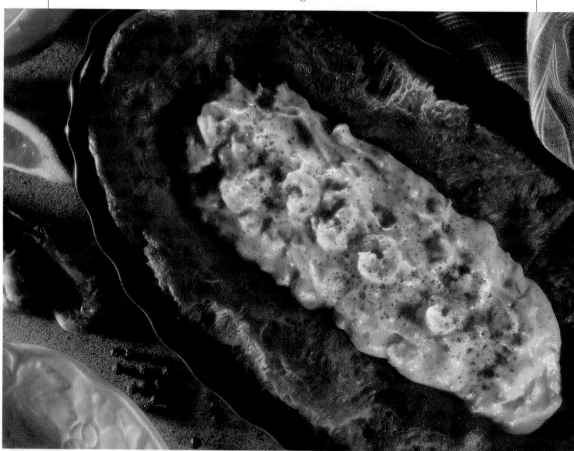

Trout à l'orange

75g (3oz) butter

4 trout fillets (100g/4oz each approx.)

½ orange, juice and grated rind

140ml (¼ pint) double cream

seasoning

Serves 4

Fruity Fish Stir Fry

50g (2oz) butter

275g (10oz) haddock fillets, cut into pieces

1 red pepper, cut into thin strips

4 spring onions, sliced

50g (2oz) peeled prawns

50g (2oz) beansprouts

100g (4oz) sweetcorn

1 teaspoon Chinese seasoning

2 tablespoons soy sauce

1 x 225g (8oz) can peach slices in juice

1 x 125g (5oz) carton natural yogurt

Serves 4

METHOD

1. Melt butter in frying pan, add orange juice and gently sauté trout for 2-3 minutes each side until cooked. Remove to a serving dish and keep warm.
2. Add cream and orange rind to butter in pan and bring to the boil. Simmer for 1-2 minutes until sauce thickens. Season.
3. Pour sauce over trout fillets and serve immediately with rice. Garnish with orange slices using remaining ½ orange.

METHOD

1. Melt the butter in a large frying pan or wok and stir fry the haddock gently for a few minutes until cooked, then remove from pan/wok.
2. Add the pepper, spring onions and stir fry 2-3 minutes. Add the prawns, beansprouts, sweetcorn and peach slices then stir in the Chinese seasoning, soy sauce and 2 tablespoons peach juice.
3. Return the haddock then add the yogurt and heat through without boiling.
4. Serve immediately with noodles or rice.

Cod & Mushroom Crumble

225g (8oz) cod fillets

100g (4oz) mushrooms, sliced and cooked

2 hard boiled eggs, chopped

1 stick celery, finely chopped

280ml (½ pint) milk

25g (1oz) butter

25g (1oz) plain flour

50g (2oz) cheddar cheese, grated

seasoning

Crumble Topping

100g (4oz) wholemeal flour

50g (2oz) butter

grated rind of 1 lemon

Oven temperature: 180°C/350°F/No. 4
Position in oven: centre
Time in oven: 20-30 minutes

Serves 4

METHOD

1. Poach fish in a little of the measured milk then drain liquid and flake fish. Add remaining milk to the liquid and slowly blend it with the flour in a saucepan.
2. Add butter and bring sauce to the boil stirring all the time. Simmer 2-3 minutes.
3. Add cheese, mushrooms, eggs and celery to sauce. Stir in flaked fish and season.
4. To make crumble, rub butter into flour, to give a breadcrumb consistency then stir in lemon rind.
5. Place fish mixture in an ovenproof casserole and cover with crumble topping.
6. Bake in oven, then serve hot with a crisp green salad and French bread.

Sole Swiss Style

4 pieces sole or whiting, filleted and washed

50g (2oz) butter

3 tablespoons chopped mixed fresh herbs
(tarragon, sage and parsley)

salt and pepper

Oven Temperature:	180°C/350°F/No. 4
Position in Oven:	centre
Time in Oven:	10 minutes or until fish is cooked

Serves 4

METHOD
1. Wash and dry fresh herbs, remove leaves
and chop them up finely.
2. Grease a baking tray liberally with butter,
than sprinkle half of the herbs on the tray.
3. Lay the fish on the tray, place knobs of
butter on top and sprinkle on the remaining
herbs.
4. Season and bake in the oven until the fish
is cooked.

Tuna & Shrimp Kedgeree

100g (4oz) brown rice

1 teaspoon mixed herbs

1 teaspoon turmeric

1 x 200g (7oz) can tuna, drained and flaked

1 x 200g (7oz) can shrimps, drained and washed

50g (2oz) butter

2 eggs, hard boiled and chopped

100g (4oz) cheddar cheese, grated

seasoning

Serves 4

METHOD
1. Cook rice with herbs and turmeric in
boiling salted water until tender. Drain and
rinse well.
2. Melt the butter in a pan, add the cooked
rice, tuna, shrimps and eggs then cook gently
for about 5 minutes until hot. Season.
3. Stir in half the cheese then place in serving
dish, sprinkle with remaining cheese and grill
to melt cheese. Serve immediately.

Rich Chocolate Pots

75g (3oz) chocolate sponge, chopped
(e.g. ½ chocolate Swiss Roll)

1 packet (69g/2½oz) chocolate dessert mix

280ml (½ pint) milk

100g (4oz) Greek style yogurt

1 tablespoon Tia Maria liqueur

25g (1oz) chocolate, finely grated

Serves 6

1. Make up dessert mix with milk.
2. In a bowl, blend yogurt and liqueur together then mix in chocolate dessert and fold in sponge.
3. Divide mixture between 6 ramekin dishes and chill well.
4. Serve, sprinkled with finely grated chocolate.

Yogurt Trifle

1 Swiss roll

1 can raspberries

280ml (½ pint) raspberry yogurt

Sherry, if liked

Serves 4

METHOD
1. Chop up Swiss roll and place in the bottom of a trifle dish.
2. Mix the juice from the raspberries with a little sherry and pour over the sponge.
3. Place raspberries on top of sponge then pour yogurt on top of fruit.
4. Decorate with a little cream and raspberries.

Raspberry Lemon Crunch

225g (8oz) raspberries, fresh or frozen

2 tablespoons lemon curd

140ml (¼ pint) cold custard

225g (8oz) Greek style yogurt

2 crunchy cereal bars

Serves 4

METHOD
1. Divide the raspberries between 4 sundae glasses.
2. Blend the lemon curd into the cold custard. Add the yogurt and mix well then spoon over the raspberries.
3. Crush the cereal bars and sprinkle over custard layer as a topping.

Strawberry Syllabub Surprise

Choux Pastry:

25g (1oz) butter

1 teaspoon caster sugar

140ml (¼ pint) milk

100g (4oz) plain flour, sieved

3 eggs, beaten

15g (½oz) flaked almonds

Syllabub:

½ orange, finely grated rind and juice

2 tablespoons brandy

2 tablespoons sherry

2 tablespoons caster sugar

280ml (½ pint) double cream

To decorate:

225g (8oz) strawberries

icing sugar

Oven Temperature:	200°C/400°F/No. 6
Position in oven:	centre
Time in oven:	35 minutes

Serves 6

METHOD
1. For the syllabub, put sherry, brandy, orange juice and rind and sugar in a bowl and leave for 2-3 hours.
2. To make choux pastry – place butter, sugar and milk in a pan and bring to the boil. Stir in the flour, remove pan from heat and beat well until dough leaves the sides of the pan. Gradually add eggs then beat until the mixture is smooth and shiny.
3. Pipe the mixture (using a piping bag fitted with a 1cm (½") star pipe) into 12 choux buns to make an 18cm (7") ring onto a greased baking tray. Sprinkle with almonds and bake until well risen and golden brown. Cool on a wire tray.
4. Remove tops of choux buns, leaving base as a complete ring and place on serving plate.
5. Add cream to syllabub mixture and whip until stiff. Pipe or spoon some syllabub on top of choux ring base then replace tops and dust with icing sugar.
6. Pipe or spoon remaining syllabub in centre of ring and decorate with strawberries.

Meringue Swans

Meringue:

| 2 egg whites |
| 100g (4oz) caster sugar |
| 150g (6oz) raspberries |
| 140ml (¼ pint) double cream, whipped |

Oven Temperature: 100°C/200°F
Position in Oven: centre
Time in Oven: 2-2½ hours

Serves 6

METHOD
1. Whisk egg whites until very stiff and dry.
Gradually add ½ the caster sugar whisking well
all the time.
2. Add remainder of caster sugar and fold in.
3. Place mixture in a piping bag with a star
pipe and pipe onto a buttered tray, six oval
shapes and then pipe round the edge to make
an oval basket.
4. Now pipe six "necks" in the shape of an S.
5. Bake in the oven till dry. Cool.
6. Fill baskets with raspberries, pipe cream
round edge of basket and place neck at one
end to form the swan.

Raspberry Cheesecake

Base:

| 100g (4oz) chocolate digestive biscuits, crushed |
| 25g (1oz) melted butter |

Filling:

| 150g (6oz) raspberries, a few to decorate |
| 50g (2oz) caster sugar |
| 100g (4oz) smooth cottage cheese |
| 140ml (¼ pint) double cream |
| 1 kiwi fruit |

Serves 6

METHOD
1. Mix ingredients for base together and press
into a 15cm (6 inch) loose bottomed cake tin.
Chill.
2. Wash raspberries and mix with caster sugar.
3. Whip up cream then mix with the cottage
cheese.
4. Combine raspberries and cream mixture
and place on top of base. Smooth out surface
and chill.
5. Decorate with kiwi fruit and raspberries.

Vanilla Dairy Ice Cream

2 eggs

2 egg yolks

75g (3oz) caster sugar

560ml (1 pint) milk

½ teaspoon vanilla essence

280ml (½ pint) double cream, lightly whipped

Serves 6-8

METHOD

1. Place the eggs, egg yolks, sugar and essence in a bowl and whisk until pale.
2. Bring the milk almost to the boil then pour over the eggs. Strain the mixture through a sieve back into the pan.

3. Cook the custard mixture gently over a low heat, stirring constantly until the mixture thickens enough to coat the back of a wooden spoon. Leave to become cool.
4. Carefully fold the lightly whipped cream into the cooled custard and spoon into ice trays or a suitable shallow freezer container and freeze for 1 hour until half frozen and mushy. Stir well and mash with a fork then re-freeze for 2-3 hours until firm.

Variations:

Omit the vanilla essence and add:

(a) 100g (4oz) grated chocolate, melted into the milk

(b) 3 tablespoons coffee essence stirred into the custard

(c) 225g (8oz) pureed raspberries or other fruit added to the custard

Raspberry Mousse

2 eggs, separated

50g (2oz) caster sugar

225g (8oz) raspberries, leave aside a few for decoration

140ml (¼ pint) double cream, whipped

2 teaspoons gelatine

3 tablespoons hot water

Serves 4-6

METHOD

1. Whisk yolks and sugar until thick and creamy.
2. Puree raspberries then fold into mixture along with whipped cream.
3. Dissolve gelatine in water and add.
4. Whisk up egg whites until stiff and fold into mixture.
5. Pour into a suitable pudding dish. Put into the fridge to set.
6. When set, decorate as liked.

Strawberry Gâteau

100g (4oz) self raising flour

4 eggs

100g (4oz) caster sugar

280ml (½ pint) whipping cream

225g (8oz) strawberries, sliced

Oven Temperature: 220°C/425°F/No. 7
Position in Oven: top half
Time in Oven: 10 minutes

Serves 8-10

METHOD
1. Whisk eggs and sugar until creamy.
2. Carefully fold in sieved flour.
3. Pour mixture into two 18cm (7 inch) buttered tins.
4. Bake in oven until cooked.
5. Place on cooling tray.
6. Whip up cream, add half the strawberries to half the cream and use to sandwich the sponge together.
7. Cover top of cake with remainder of cream and decorate with remaining strawberries.

Favourite Bread and Butter Pudding

8 slices bread, well buttered, crusts removed

50g (2oz) sultanas

grated rind of 1 orange

50g (2oz) brown sugar

280ml (½ pint) milk

1 egg

Oven temperature: 180°C/350°F/No. 4
Position in oven: centre
Time in oven: 45-50 minutes

Serves 4

METHOD

1. Butter a ¾ litre (1½ pint) pie dish.
2. Cut bread slices into 3 and arrange half the bread buttered side down in the dish.
3. Cover with half the orange rind, half the sugar and sultanas. Cover with remaining bread.
4. Sprinkle with the remaining ingredients.
5. Mix egg and milk together, pour over the pudding. Leave to soak for at least 30 minutes and bake until golden brown.

St. Clement's Slice

| 225g (8oz) oatmeal biscuits, crushed |
| 50g (2oz) butter |
| 140ml (¼ pint) double cream |
| 25g (1oz) icing sugar |
| 1 orange, rind and juice |
| 1 lemon, rind and juice |
| 225g (8oz) Greek style yogurt |
| 4 trifle sponges, crumbled |

To Decorate:

| fresh orange and lemon slices |

Serves 6-8

METHOD

1. Melt butter and mix with biscuits. Line a 1kg(2lb) loaf tin with cling film, sprinkle half the biscuits into the base and press down well.
2. Whip the cream and sugar together until stiff then add finely grated orange and lemon rind.
3. Strain the orange and lemon juice and stir into the cream. Fold in the yogurt then add crumbled sponges and mix evenly.
4. Spread cream mixture over the biscuit base then finish with remaining biscuits. Freeze until firm.
5. Remove from freezer 30 minutes before serving to allow slice to soften slightly.
6. Turn out, remove cling film and serve decorated with orange and lemon slices.

Fresh Fruit Flan

| 1 large 200g (7oz) bought sponge flan case |

Filling:

| 1 egg yolk |
| 25g (1oz) caster sugar |
| 15g (½oz) plain flour |
| ½ teaspoon vanilla or almond essence |
| 140ml (¼ pint) milk |

Topping:

| fresh fruit – selection of strawberries, raspberries, grapes, kiwi fruit or pineapple |
| apricot jam to glaze |
| 140ml (¼ pint) double cream, whipped |

Serves 6-8

METHOD

1. Beat egg yolk and sugar together in a pan then gradually blend in flour, essence and milk. Bring to the boil stirring all the time until mixture thickens then cook for 2-3 minutes. Allow to cool.
2. When custard is almost cold, use it to fill the sponge flan case.
3. Cover custard with a selection of fresh fruit then brush with melted apricot jam to glaze fruit.
4. Allow glaze to cool and set then decorate by piping cream around flan.

Tipsy Tartan Trifle

4 slices sponge cake	
50g (2oz) ratafia biscuits	
4 tablespoons sweet sherry	
225g (8oz) raspberries, frozen or canned	
2 tablespoons custard powder	
1 tablespoon sugar	
560ml (1 pint) milk	
2 teaspoons finely grated lemon rind	
280ml (½ pint) double cream, whipped	

To decorate:

1 pack of red, blue & green decorating gel.

Serves 6-8

METHOD

1. Arrange sponge in base of glass serving dish. Crumble ratafias over sponge, pour on sherry then place raspberries on top.
2. Make custard with custard powder, sugar and milk then blend in lemon rind and pour over raspberries. Leave until cold.
3. Spread whipped cream over custard and decorate with coloured decorating gel to give a tartan effect.

Frosted Christmas Pud

150g(6oz) mixed dried fruit
50g(2oz) glacé cherries, chopped
2 tablespoons brandy
2 level tablespoons custard powder
1 level tablespoon sugar
280ml (½ pint) milk
50g(2oz) plain chocolate, grated
280ml(½ pint) double cream, whipped

Serves 6

METHOD

1. Place mixed fruit and cherries in a bowl, add brandy and soak for 30 minutes.
2. Mix custard powder and sugar with a little milk. Heat remaining milk and make custard. Leave to become cold.
3. Add fruit mixture and grated chocolate to cold custard and mix through.
4. Fold whipped cream into custard mixture and spoon into a ¾ litre (1½ pt) pudding basin or mould lined with clingfilm.
5. Freeze for 2-3 hours until firm.
6. Remove from freezer about ½ hour before turning out to serve.

Yule Log

Sponge:

2 large eggs	
50g (2oz) caster sugar	
40g (1½oz) self raising flour	*sieved together*
15g (½oz) cocoa powder	
1 dessertspoon warm water	

Filling:

140ml (¼ pint) double cream
100g (4oz) sweetened chestnut puree

Icing:

50g (2oz) butter
100g (4oz) icing sugar, sieved
1 tablespoon cocoa powder
1 tablespoon milk

Oven temperature:	220°C/425°F/No. 7
Position in oven:	centre
Time in oven:	7-10 minutes

Serves 6-8

METHOD

1. Grease and line a 30 x 20cm (12 x 8 inch) swiss roll tin.
2. Whisk eggs and sugar together in a bowl until light and creamy.
3. Carefully fold in flour and cocoa powder then fold in water.
4. Pour into prepared tin and bake until well risen and firm.
5. Turn out onto a sheet of sugared greaseproof paper resting on a damp tea towel. Carefully remove base paper and roll up. Leave to become cold.
6. To make the filling, whip the cream then blend in the sweetened chestnut puree. Unroll cold swiss roll, spread with filling then carefully roll up again.
7. To make the icing, cream the butter, gradually blend in the icing sugar and cocoa powder then add milk and beat well.
8. Cover swiss roll completely with butter icing then use a fork to make lines that look like bark. Serve chilled with a Christmas decoration or holly on top.

Apple and Sultana Tart

Serves 4-6

225g (8oz) plain flour

pinch salt

150g (6oz) butter, cubed

1 tablespoon caster sugar

1 egg yolk

cold water to bind

2 green eating apples

1 tablespoon lemon juice

1 tablespoon caster sugar

1 tablespoon sultanas

140ml (¼ pint) double cream

2 eggs, lightly beaten

2 teaspoons vanilla essence

1 teaspoon ground cinnamon

½ teaspoon ground cloves

lemon rind

Oven temperature: 190°C/375°F/No. 5
Position in oven: centre
Time in oven: 45 minutes

METHOD
1. Sift the flour with salt.
2. Rub butter into flour until the mixture resembles fine breadcrumbs.
3. Stir in sugar, egg yolk and enough water to bind the mixture to a firm dough, chill in refrigerator for 30 minutes.
4. Peel, core and half the apples. Slice the apples thinly, keeping each half in shape and sprinkle with lemon juice.
5. Roll out pastry to fit a 23cm (9") flan dish.
6. Arrange the apples in the flan, sprinkle the sugar over the apples and bake in oven for 15 minutes.
7. Meanwhile, mix cream, eggs, essence and spices together.
8. Sprinkle sultanas in base of flan and pour the cream mixture carefully around the apples. Bake for a further 30 minutes.
9. Decorate with sieved icing sugar and lemon rind. Serve hot or cold.

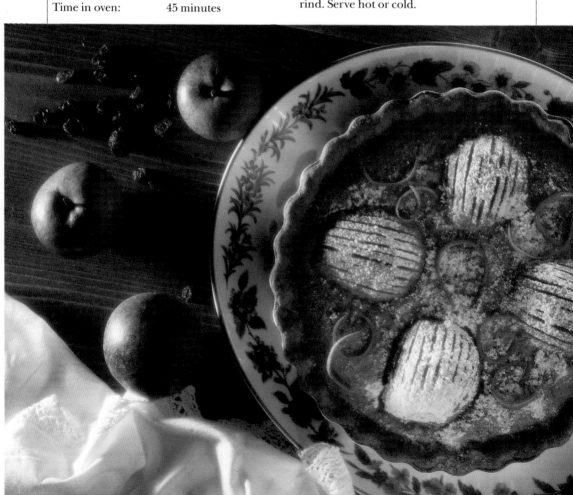

Blackcurrant Cheesecake

Base:

100g (4oz) oatmeal biscuits, crushed

50g (2oz) butter

Filling:

1 packet (69g/2½oz) vanilla dessert mix

280ml (½ pint) milk

100g (4oz) smooth cottage cheese

½ lemon, grated

Topping:

½ x 400g (14oz) can blackcurrant fruit filling

Serves 4-6

METHOD

1. To make base – melt butter, add biscuit crumbs and mix well. Press into a 20cm (8") loose bottomed cake tin. Chill.
2. Make up dessert mix with milk.
3. Put soft cheese in a bowl, mix in lemon rind then gradually whisk in milk pudding until smooth.
4. Spoon the mixture over the base and chill for 2 hours until set.
5. Remove from tin and spread fruit filling over top.

Chocolate Orange Surprise

100g (4oz) bar milk chocolate

100g (4oz) butter

75g (3oz) caster sugar

4 tablespoons whisky

1 orange, grated rind and juice

280ml (½ pint) double cream

Serves 6-8

METHOD

1. Melt chocolate with butter and sugar in a bowl over a pan of hot water. Leave to cool.
2. Stir in whisky, orange rind and juice.
3. Add cream and whip until thick.
3. Place in glasses and serve chilled with petticoat tails.

Manhattan Pie

50g (2oz) butter, melted
100g (4oz) chocolate cookies, finely crushed
450g (1lb) smooth cottage cheese
75g (3oz) icing sugar
1 egg, beaten
2 tablespoons green creme de menthe
1 teaspoon white creme de cacao
100g (4oz) milk cooking chocolate
50g (2oz) soured cream

Oven temperature: 180°C/350°F/No. 4
Position in oven: centre
Time in oven: 40 minutes

Serves 4-6

Magic Lemon Pudding

1 lemon, grated rind and juice
50g (2oz) butter
100g (4oz) caster sugar
2 eggs, separated
50g (2oz) self raising flour
280ml (½ pint) milk

Oven Temperature: 180°C/350°F/No. 4
Position in Oven: centre
Time in Oven: 40-45 minutes

Serves 4-6

METHOD
1. Stir the butter into the crushed biscuits. Press firmly into the bottom of a 20cm (8") loose bottomed cake tin.
2. In a large bowl, beat cottage cheese, icing sugar, egg, creme de menthe and creme de cacao together until smooth.
3. Pour over biscuit base and bake. Allow to cool.
4. Melt chocolate over a pan of water on a very low heat. When melted, remove from heat and stir in soured cream. Spread over the cheesecake. Refrigerate at least 5 hours before serving.

METHOD
1. Cream butter and sugar together with lemon rind.
2. Add beaten yolks and a little flour. Stir in milk, strained lemon juice and remaining sieved flour alternately.
3. Whisk whites until stiff and fold into mixture then pour into a buttered souffle dish and bake.

The pudding gives a light sponge topping and a tangy lemon sauce underneath and is delicious served with cream or custard.

Apple and Cinnamon Pancakes

100g (4oz) plain flour, sieved

pinch of salt

1 egg

280ml (½ pint) milk

seasoning

4 large eating apples, peeled, cored and sliced

½ teaspoon cinnamon

100g (4oz) demerara sugar

75g (3oz) butter

Serves 4

METHOD
1. Sieve flour and salt.
2. Add egg and a little milk and beat well.
3. Gradually add remainder of milk – leave for ½ hour.
4. Pour a little batter into a hot frying pan brushed with melted butter.
5. When batter is set and underside brown, turn and brown second side. Turn onto greaseproof paper. Make 7 other pancakes.
6. In a saucepan, gently cook apples, half the cinnamon and sugar and 50g (2oz) butter for 20 minutes or until apples are tender, stirring occasionally.
7. Lay pancake flat, spoon on some of the filling and roll up. Fill rest of pancakes.

8. In a large frying pan, melt remaining butter, sugar and cinnamon and fry pancakes on both sides until golden brown.
9. Place pancakes on a plate and cover with cinnamon mixture. Serve with dairy ice cream or cream.

Apricot and Mango Creams

140ml (¼ pint) carton double cream

2 x 125g (5oz) cartons apricot and mango yogurt

2 teaspoons demerara sugar

Serves 4

METHOD
1. Whip up double cream in a bowl.
2. Add yogurt to cream.
3. Divide into four tall glasses.
4. Shake ½ teaspoon demerara sugar on top of each sweet. Serve chilled.

Devil's Food Cake

100g (4oz) butter	
225g (8oz) soft dark brown sugar	
225g (8oz) plain flour	
1 teaspoon bicarbonate of soda	*sieved together*
50g (2oz) drinking chocolate powder	
2 eggs, beaten	
225ml (8fl.oz) milk	

Frosting:

100g (4oz) plain chocolate
25g (1oz) butter
85ml (3fl.oz) milk
340g (12oz) icing sugar, sieved

Filling:

140ml (¼ pint) double cream, whipped

Oven temperature: 180°C/350°F/No. 4
Position in oven: centre
Time in oven: 30-40 minutes

Serves 8

METHOD

1. Butter and line two 20cm (8") round sandwich tins.
2. To make sponge: cream the butter and sugar together in a bowl.
3. Add eggs, milk and flour alternately, beating well.
4. Divide mixture between prepared tins and bake in oven until firm and sponge has shrunk slightly from sides of tins. Cool on a wire tray.
5. To make frosting: Place chocolate, butter and milk in a pan and melt over a low heat. Remove from heat, add icing sugar and beat well. Leave to become cold.
6. Cut the sponges in half and sandwich each together with whipped double cream then sandwich the two cream filled sponges together with some of the chocolate frosting.
7. Cover the cake completely with remaining frosting to give an attractive finish.

Sugar Plum Pie

450g (1lb) plums, stones removed

140ml (¼ pint) water

75g (3oz) sugar

100g (4oz) sponge cake, broken into pieces

4 tablespoons cornflour

2 tablespoons caster sugar

2 eggs, separated

560ml (1 pint) milk

100g (4oz) caster sugar

Oven temperature: 180°C/350°F/No. 4
Position in oven: centre
Time in oven: 10-15 minutes

Serves 4-6

METHOD
1. Place plums, water and sugar in a large pan and cook gently until the plums are soft.
2. Place sponge cake pieces in a 1.1 litre (2 pint) ovenproof dish and cover with strained plums.
3. Blend cornflour, sugar, egg yolks and three tablespoons milk together. Heat the remaining milk and add to mixture, stirring continuously over a low heat until sauce thickens.
4. Pour custard over plums.
5. Whisk up egg whites until they stand in peaks. Whisk in half the sugar and fold in the remainder – spoon meringue over custard. Bake and serve warm.

Mandarin Crème Brûlée

1 x 425g (15oz) can mandarin orange segments, drained

2 tablespoons Cointreau

280ml (½ pint) double cream

50g-75g (2-3oz) soft brown sugar

To serve:

Langue de chat biscuits

Serves 4

METHOD
1. Reserve a few mandarins for decoration then divide the mandarins between 4 ramekin dishes. Sprinkle Cointreau over mandarins.
2. Whip double cream stiffly then cover fruit completely with cream.
3. Sprinkle each dessert with a thin layer of brown sugar that completely covers the cream.
4. Place under a very hot grill until the sugar turns to caramel.
5. Chill for about 1 hour.
6. Serve topped with a few mandarins and accompanied by biscuits.

BAKING

Sticky Gingerbread

150g (6oz) butter	

150g (6oz) butter
225g (8oz) soft brown sugar
4 tablespoons treacle
6 tablespoons golden syrup
2 tablespoons honey
450g (1lb) plain flour
3 teaspoons baking powder
1 teaspoon bicarbonate of soda
½ teaspoon salt
2 teaspoons ground ginger
1 teaspoon cinnamon
280ml (½ pint) milk
1 large egg

To decorate:

1 x butter icing recipe (Dad's Day Cake Page 71)
toasted flaked almonds

Oven temperature: 180°C/350°F/No. 4
Position oven: centre
Time in oven: 1½ hours

METHOD
1. Grease and line a 20cm (8") square cake tin.
2. Melt butter, sugar, treacle, syrup and honey together in a pan.
3. Sieve flour, baking powder, bicarbonate of soda, salt and spices together in a bowl.
4. Beat egg and milk together and add to flour along with the treacle mixture. Beat well until smooth then pour mixture into cake tin and bake in oven until well risen and a skewer comes our clean from the centre.
5. Cool in tin then turn out onto a wire tray.
6. Store gingerbread for 2-4 days before decorating with butter icing and toasted flaked almonds.

Spicy Shortbread Biscuits

150g (6oz) plain flour
pinch salt
2 teaspoons mixed spice
100g (4oz) butter
50g (2oz) caster sugar
demerara sugar

Oven temperature: 160°C/310°F/No. 2½
Position in oven: centre
Time in oven: 40 minutes

METHOD
1. Add salt and spice to flour.
2. Cream butter and sugar together in a bowl. Gradually work the flour into the creamed mixture and knead until smooth.
3. Form mixture into a sausage shape 15cm (6") long.
4. Roll in demerara sugar then cut with a sharp knife into twelve 1cm (½") slices and place on a greased baking tray.
5. Prick biscuits with a fork and bake in oven.
6. Sprinkle with demerara sugar and cool on a wire tray.

Chocolate Shortbread Biscuits
Make shortbread biscuits as above then dip the base of each biscuit in melted plain or milk cooking chocolate and leave to set on a wire tray.

Orange Blossom Cake

150g (6oz) butter
175g (7oz) caster sugar
5 eggs, beaten
175g (7oz) plain flour
100g (4oz) cornflour   } sieved together
4 teaspoons baking powder
4 tablespoons milk
150g (6oz) mandarin oranges

Oven temperature: 160°C/310°F/No. 2½
Position in oven: centre
Time in oven: 2 hours

METHOD
1. Cream butter and sugar together until light and fluffy.
2. Add eggs alternately with the flour beating well after each addition.
3. Stir in the milk and mandarin oranges. Leave aside a few mandarin oranges for decoration.
4. Spoon the mixture into a well greased 23cm (9") cake tin and bake.
5. When cake is cooked, cool before turning out. Decorate with water icing and mandarin oranges. Dust lightly with icing sugar just before serving.

Spicy Oat Fingers

225g (8oz) butter	
225g (8oz) soft brown sugar	
6 level tablespoons syrup	
450g (1lb) porridge oats	
1 teaspoon cinnamon	
1 teaspoon ground ginger	
100g (4oz) raisins	

Topping

100g (4oz) butter	
150g (6oz) icing sugar, sieved	
1 teaspoon ground ginger	
1 tablespoon orange rind	
2 tablespoons orange juice	
3 tablespoons double cream	

Spicy Milk Loaf

450g (1lb) self raising flour	
¼ teaspoon salt	
1 teaspoon cinnamon	
¼ teaspoon ground ginger	
1 teaspoon mixed spice	
150g (6oz) mixed dried fruit	
100g (4oz) soft brown sugar	
2 tablespoons honey	
75g (3oz) butter	
280ml (½ pint) milk	

Oven temperature: 170°C/325°F/No. 3
Position in oven: centre
Time in oven: 1 hour approx.

Oven Temperature: 180°C/350°F/No. 4
Position in oven: centre
Time in oven: 25 minutes
Makes 24 approx

METHOD
1. Place butter, sugar and syrup together over a low heat.
2. Stir in the oats, cinnamon, ginger and raisins.
3. Place mixture into a lightly greased swiss roll tin and flatten slightly. Bake.
4. Topping – Cream butter, then gradually add icing sugar and ginger a little at a time.
5. Stir in the orange rind, juice and cream.
6. Spread topping over biscuit base and cut into portions.

METHOD
1. Line and grease a 1kg (2lb) loaf tin.
2. Sieve flour, salt and spices together then stir in dried fruit.
3. Put sugar, honey and butter in a pan and heat gently until melted then mix with the milk into the flour to give a fairly sticky consistency.
4. Turn the mixture into the prepared tin and bake in oven until a skewer inserted in the centre comes out cleanly.

Marshmallow Fudge Bars

4 tablespoons golden syrup

75g (3oz) butter

75g (3oz) milk cooking chocolate, broken into pieces and melted

225g (8oz) digestive biscuits, coarsely crushed

50g (2oz) marshmallows, chopped

50g (2oz) glacé cherries, quartered

50g (2oz) sultanas

To decorate:

150g (6oz) white chocolate

glacé cherries

METHOD

1. Gently heat syrup and butter together in a saucepan until butter has melted. Stir well.
2. Remove pan from heat, add chocolate and stir vigorously until well blended.
3. Stir in biscuit crumbs, marshmallows, cherries and sultanas. Mix well.
4. Spread evenly into an 18cm (7") square cake tin lined with greaseproof paper. Chill until set.
5. Cover with melted chocolate, decorate with cherries and cut into bars.

Choc Chip Chunks

100g (4oz) butter

3 tablespoons honey

1 tablespoon drinking chocolate powder

225g (8oz) chocolate chip cookies, crushed

50g (2oz) raisins

Topping:

150g (6oz) milk cooking chocolate

40g (1½oz) butter

1 tablespoon milk

METHOD

1. Melt butter and honey in a pan. Add chocolate powder, biscuits and raisins and mix well.
2. Press into a 30 x 20cm (12 x 8 inch) swiss roll tin lined with clingfilm and chill until firm.
3. Melt topping ingredients in a bowl over gently simmering water then pour over mixture, spreading evenly.
4. When set remove from tin and cut into chunks.

Easter Biscuits

100g (4oz) butter, softened
100g (4oz) caster sugar
1 egg yolk
225g (8oz) plain flour
50g (2oz) sultanas
25g (1oz) glacé cherries, chopped
4 tablespoons milk

To make glaze:

1 egg white, lightly beaten
caster sugar

Oven temperature:	160°C/310°F/No. 2½
Position in oven:	centre
Time in oven:	15-20 minutes

METHOD
1. Cream butter and sugar until light and fluffy. Beat in egg yolk and fold in flour, sultanas and cherries.
2. Gradually add milk, mixing well until mixture forms a stiff dough.
3. Roll out to about 3mm (⅛") thick and cut twenty four 5cm (2") rounds. Place on a baking tray and bake in oven.
4. After 10 minutes, remove tray from oven, brush biscuits with egg white and sprinkle on sugar. Return to oven at the same temperature for a further 5-10 minutes.
5. Remove biscuits from tray and place on a wire tray to cool.

Family Fruit Cake

150g (6oz) soft brown sugar
150g (6oz) butter
340g (12oz) self raising flour
1 teaspoon mixed spice
3 eggs
4 tablespoons milk
250g (9oz) mixed dried fruit

Oven Temperature:	150°C/300°F/No. 2
Position in Oven:	centre
Time in Oven:	1½ hours

METHOD
1. Butter and line a 20cm (8") deep cake tin.
2. Cream butter and sugar well.
3. Add flour with mixed spice through it and milk with eggs beaten into it, alternately.
4. Add mixed fruit and mix thoroughly. Bake.

Easter Flower Cake

450g (1lb) white marzipan	
150g (6oz) butter	
150g (6oz) caster sugar	
225g (8oz) plain flour	
pinch salt	sieved together
1 teaspoon cinnamon	
3 eggs	
140ml (¼ pint) milk	
225g (8oz) currants	
100g (4oz) sultanas	
100g (4oz) glacé cherries, quartered	
2 tablespoons apricot jam, strained	
crystallised flowers and ribbon to decorate	

Oven Temperature:	150°C/300°F/No. 2
Position in oven:	centre
Time in oven:	2½/3 hours

METHOD
1. Grease and line an 18cm (7") or 20cm (8") cake tin.
2. Cream butter and sugar until light and fluffy then alternately add sieved dry ingredients with eggs.
3. Stir in milk and fruit.
4. Spread half of the mixture in the base of the prepared tin.
5. Roll out about one third of the marzipan and trim to fit the cake tin. Place the marzipan circle on cake mixture and cover with rest of mixture. Bake. Once cooked, leave to cool in tin.
6. Roll just over half the remaining marzipan to fit top of cake. Brush cake with jam and place marzipan on top. Fork the edges and score the top.
7. Use the remaining marzipan to make 8 even sized balls. Arrange on cake, sticking them down with dots of jam. Place cake under grill until marzipan begins to brown.
8. Decorate cake with crystallised flowers and ribbon.

To make Crystallised Flowers
Brush fresh flower heads with egg white then sprinkle with caster sugar and allow to dry on a wire tray for 1 hour.

Mother's Day Cake

Sponge:

150g (6oz) butter	
75g (3oz) caster sugar	
75g (3oz) soft brown sugar	
150g (6oz) self raising flour	
½ teaspoon ground ginger	*sieved together*
½ teaspoon mixed spice	
1 tablespoon instant coffee powder	
3 eggs, beaten	
25g (1oz) sultanas	
3 tablespoons milk	

Decoration:

450g (1lb) fondant
pink food colouring
apricot jam, melted and sieved
25cm (10") square silver cake board
20cm (8") thin square silver cake board
1 metre lilac ribbon
100g (4oz) sugared almonds
white or pink mini bow

Oven temperature: 180°C/350°F/No. 4
Position in oven: centre
Time in oven: 50 minutes

METHOD
1. Grease and line the base of a 1kg (2lb) loaf tin.

2. Cream butter and sugars well together until smooth and golden, add flour and eggs alternately, beating well then stir in sultanas and milk and place in prepared tin.
3. Bake until firm and golden then cool on a wire tray. Transfer cake to cake board and brush with jam.
4. Shape a small piece of fondant to make a gift card 5cm squared (2 inch squared) leave to dry. Colour rest of fondant pale pink then roll out and completely cover cake. This uses about half of the fondant.
5. Cut the thin silver cake board in half (or use stiff card) for the lid. Roll out remaining fondant and cover the underside of cake board with fondant. This uses about 100g (4oz) fondant. Use a knife to mark diagonal lines on the cake sides and lid.
6. Use a little fondant and make an edging and attach with water to top of cake. Leave to dry for 24 hours.
7. Write a message on fondant gift card using an icing pen (pink) and attach to lid with water. (Alternatively you could use a bought gift card). Decorate with a mini bow.
8. Finish cake with ribbon then put sugared almonds on top and place lid at an angle over almonds.

NOTE: This cake is also ideal as a Birthday Cake in which case, write a Birthday message on gift card and add some candles. Mum's favourite chocolates could be used instead of almonds.

Dad's Day Cake

Sponge:.

100g (4oz) butter	
100g (4oz) caster sugar	
2 eggs, beaten	
½ teaspoon vanilla essence	
100g (4oz) self raising flour	*sieved together*
1 teaspoon baking powder	

Butter Icing:

50g (2oz) butter
100g (4oz) icing sugar, sieved
1 tablespoon milk

225g (8oz) fondant
drinking chocolate powder or brown food colouring

Oven Temperature:	180°C/350°F/No. 4
Position in Oven:	centre
Time in Oven:	35 - 40 minutes

METHOD

1. Grease and line two 10cm (4") diameter washed out food cans.
2. To make sponge: Cream softened butter and sugar well together then gradually beat in eggs, flour and essence. Beat mixture for 2-3 minutes until smooth and glossy then divide between prepared cans.
3. Bake until golden, allow to cool for 5 minutes then turn out on wire tray.
4. To assemble cake: Sandwich sponges, one on top of the other with a little butter icing. Cover sponges completely with a thin layer of butter icing.
5. Colour ⅔ fondant icing brown by kneading drinking chocolate powder into the icing. Roll out fondant on a surface dusted with icing sugar and cover sponges around the side only. Use some fondant to make a handle which is best secured with cocktail sticks. Any remaining brown fondant can be rolled out to make a cigar.
6. Cover top of tankard roughly with remaining butter icing to look like froth, using a fork.
7. Roll out remaining white fondant icing and cut out an oval plaque. Pipe with chocolate butter icing or use an icing pen to write a message (alternatively, cut a plaque from white cardboard and write your message neatly in felt tip pen). Attach plaque to front of tankard using a little butter icing.

This cake is also ideal as a Birthday Cake in which case candles can be added to the top.

Mickey & Minnie Cakes

Sponge:

150g (6oz) self raising flour	*sieved together*
½ teaspoon baking powder	
125g (5oz) caster sugar	
25g (1oz) butter, melted	
1 x 125g (5oz) carton toffee yogurt	
2 eggs, beaten	

Decoration:

1 x butter icing recipe (see page 71)
raspberry jam
apricot jam, melted and sieved
450g (1lb) fondant
food colours: black, blue, yellow, red or pink
25cm (10") round silver cake board
1½ metres blue ribbon (optional)

Tracing Template of Mickey or Minnie Mouse

Oven Temperature:	180°C/350°F/No. 4
Position in oven:	centre
Time in oven:	35 minutes

METHOD

1. Put all the ingredients in a bowl and mix well until smooth.

2. Divide the mixture between 2 buttered 20cm (8") sandwich tins and bake in oven until golden brown.

3. Sandwich sponges together with half the butter icing and a little raspberry jam, then place on cake board and brush all over with apricot jam.

4. Roll out fondant to a circle 7.5cm (3") larger than top of cake and completely cover cake. This uses about 275g (10oz) fondant. While fondant is still soft, place greaseproof template on top of cake and gently trace over with a blunt pencil to transfer outline onto cake. Leave to dry for 24 hours.

5. Using a very fine paint brush paint over outline in black food colour. Allow to dry then paint on colours as photograph.

6. Colour remaining butter icing blue/pink then pipe small stars (No. 5 pipe) around top and bottom edge of cake. Alternatively finish with ribbon.

7. Using a No. 2 pipe, pipe Birthday Greetings on board and finish with candles.

N.B. Templates can be made by tracing a picture onto greaseproof paper – if necessary use squared paper to scale it up or down.

Oatmeal Scones

225g (8oz) self raising flour
1 teaspoon salt
50g (2oz) butter
50g (2oz) medium oatmeal
25g (1oz) caster sugar
140ml (¼ pint) milk

Oven temperature:	230°C/450°F/No. 8
Position in oven:	centre
Time in oven:	10 minutes

METHOD
1. Sieve flour and salt together in a bowl then rub in butter.
2. Stir in oatmeal and sugar, then add milk and mix to a soft dough with a knife.
3. Roll out dough, on a lightly floured surface, to 1cm (½ inch) thick round.
4. Cut out 16-18 rounds using a 5cm (2 inch) fluted cutter.

Hot Cross Buns

140ml (¼ pint) milk
25g (1oz) sugar
1 tablespoon dried yeast
225g (8oz) plain flour
1 level teaspoon salt
1 teaspoon mixed spice
½ teaspoon cinnamon
25g (1oz) butter
50g (2oz) currants
1 egg, beaten
25g (1oz) shortcrust pastry

To make glaze:

2 tablespoons caster sugar
2 tablespoons water

Oven temperature:	220°C/425°F/No. 7
Position in oven:	centre
Time in oven:	15 - 20 minutes

5. Place on a greased baking tray, brush scone tops with additional milk and bake in oven until risen and golden brown.
6. Cool on a wire tray and serve with honeyed butter.

Honeyed Butter

50g (2oz) butter
1 dessertspoon honey

METHOD
Cream butter in a bowl, then blend in honey and spread on scones.

METHOD
1. Warm milk to blood heat, stir in sugar and yeast. Leave in a warm place for 20-30 minutes or follow yeast packet directions.
2. Sieve flour, salt and spices together in a bowl then rub in butter. Stir in currants. Add yeast mixture and egg to the flour, mix to an elastic dough.
3. Knead until smooth and divide into 8 equal sized pieces. Shape each into a round bun. Place well apart on a lightly buttered tray. Cover and leave to rise for 20 minutes.
4. Cut a cross on top of each bun. Place shortcrust pastry on top to form a cross then bake in oven.
5. Dissolve caster sugar in water. Simmer until syrupy. Brush over hot buns, repeat to give shiny glazed finish.
6. Serve warm, split and buttered.

Old Macdonald's Farm

1 x Sticky Gingerbread recipe (see page 65)

2 x butter icing recipe (see page 71)

5 chocolate flakes

cotton wool

675g (1½ lbs) fondant icing

food colouring

liquorice allsorts, dolly mixtures, fondant flowers

icing for piping

desiccated coconut

coloured paper to make a duck pond

1 large cake board 35cm (14") square

METHOD

1. House is made by cutting a 7.5cm (3") slice of the cake.

2. Cut this 7.5cm (3") slice in half diagonally for the two halves of the roof.

3. Spread the sides of the house with butter icing.

4. Sandwich the two halves of the roof together with a little butter icing, spread the top of the house with butter icing and place on sloping roof.

5. Spread the roof with butter icing and cover with small pieces of chocolate flakes, leaving a small piece for a chimney. Use cotton wool to make smoke.

6. Use square liquorice allsorts or coloured fondant squares for windows and a large fondant square for a door. Attach to cake with icing once fondant is dry.

7. Use either fondant flowers or dolly mixtures as flower heads and attach to cake with icing.

8. To make grass, colour coconut with green food colouring. Brush egg white over the board and sprinkle with coconut. Attach duck pond to board with icing and surround with flowers.

9. For farm animals, mould into shape using coloured fondant. Allow to dry before drawing faces with food colouring pens.

Speedy Mice

1 tablespoon cocoa powder
40g (1½oz) ground rice
50g (2oz) caster sugar
280ml (½ pint) milk
100g (4oz) desiccated coconut
25g (1oz) marshmallows, chopped
2 tablespoons single cream
50g (2oz) cake crumbs
fondant, coloured with food colouring
coloured balls
silver ribbon

METHOD
1. Place cocoa, rice and 25g (1oz) sugar in a saucepan. Blend into a smooth paste with a little of the milk then add remaining milk.
2. Bring to boil, simmer for 10 minutes.
3. Add 25g (1oz) coconut. Transfer mixture to a large bowl. Allow to cool.
4. Mix in marshmallows, single cream, cake crumbs, sugar and a further 25g (1oz) coconut.
5. Roll the mixture out into small ovals with a pointed end for a head. Chill for ½ hour.
6. Roll ovals in remaining coconut.
7. Use coloured balls for eyes, nose, coloured fondant for ears, and ribbon for tails.

Slowly Snail

Cut 12 rounds each of brown and white bread using a 5cm (2") diameter biscuit cutter. Spread with butter. Sandwich bread together with grated cheese. Assemble the bread in the shape of a long snail, use glacé cherries and cucumber for the face, with savoury sticks for the antennae.
For the shell, stick cubed cheddar cheese, grapes and cherries onto a grapefruit with cocktail sticks.

Tropical Shake

100g (4oz) fromage frais

140ml (¼ pint) mixed citrus drink (e.g. Five Alive)

Serves 1

METHOD
1. Whisk mixed citrus juice into fromage frais.
2. Serve chilled in a glass.

Strawberry Milk Punch

125g (5oz) carton strawberry yogurt

140ml (¼ pint) chilled milk

1 scoop strawberry dairy ice cream

Serves 1

METHOD
1. Stir yogurt and milk together.
2. Whisk in softened ice cream.
3. Serve in a chilled glass.

Berry Frais

2 x 60g (2½oz) cartons blackberry & raspberry fromage frais

140ml (¼ pint) milk

Serves 1

METHOD
1. Whisk fromage frais and milk together in a jug.
2. Pour into a tall glass and serve.

Cola Fizz

140ml (¼ pint) cold milk

140ml (¼ pint) cola drink

1 scoop ice cream

Serves 1

METHOD
1. Mix milk and cola together.
2. Add ice cream and liquidise for 1-2 minutes until thick then serve in a tall glass.

Spiced Honey Mallow Float

420ml (¾ pint) milk

1 dessertspoon honey

1 teaspoon ground cinnamon

To serve

4 marshmallows

Serves 2

METHOD

1. Heat milk in a saucepan then stir in honey and cinnamon.
2. Serve hot in mugs or glasses topped with 2 marshmallows.

Whisky Liqueur Coffee

2 teaspoons brown sugar

4 tablespoons whisky liqueur

280ml (½ pint) hot black coffee

140ml (¼ pint) double cream

Serves 2

METHOD

1. Rinse two heat resistant glasses with hot water and dry well. This helps to keep the coffee hot.
2. Put sugar in glasses, add whisky liqueur then pour on coffee and stir well to dissolve sugar.
3. Pour cream over a teaspoon on top of coffee. Serve immediately.

Tomato Tipple

280ml (½ pint) tomato juice, well chilled

dash Worcester sauce

seasoning

140ml (¼ pint) cold milk

Serves 2

METHOD

1. Add Worcester sauce and seasoning to tomato juice in a jug.
2. Blend in milk and serve in glasses.

Choc-O-Cino

280ml (½ pint) milk

4 teaspoons drinking chocolate powder

Serves 2

METHOD

1. Heat milk in a saucepan then stir in 3 teaspoons chocolate powder.
2. Liquidise for 1-2 minutes until frothy then divide between 2 cups and sprinkle with rest of drinking chocolate.

SAUCES

Yogurt Dressing

140ml (¼ pint) yogurt

1 tablespoon vinegar

1 tablespoon onion, finely chopped

pinch salt

¼ teaspoon sugar

METHOD
1. Mix all the ingredients together.
2. Serve dressing with fish.

Marie Rose Sauce

140ml (¼ pint) double cream

2 tablespoons mayonnaise

2 tablespoons tomato ketchup

seasoning

METHOD
1. Lightly whip double cream.
2. Add mayonnaise and tomato ketchup.
3. Season and serve over prawns or shrimps.

Confectioner's Custard

100g (4oz) caster sugar

50g (2oz) plain flour

15g (½oz) cornflour

2 large eggs, beaten

½ teaspoon vanilla essence

560ml (1 pint) milk

50g (2oz) butter

METHOD
1. Blend the sugar, flour, cornflour, eggs and essence together in a bowl.
2. Warm the milk and stir into the sugar mixture. Return mixture to pan and cook over a low heat, stirring all the time until it thickens and just comes to the boil.
3. Remove pan from heat and blend in the butter.
4. Transfer to a bowl and leave until cold. To prevent a skin forming place 2 tablespoons milk on top of custard. Use chilled to fill cakes, flans, pastries or choux buns and éclairs.

Chocolate Sauce

75g (3oz) plain cooking chocolate
140ml (¼ pint) milk
50g (2oz) soft brown sugar

METHOD
1. Melt the chocolate with half the milk in a pan over a low heat.
2. Once chocolate is melted, add sugar and remaining milk and heat gently stirring occasionally until sugar is dissolved.
3. Simmer for 10 minutes until the sauce is thick and syrupy. Serve with profiteroles (see step by step section) or over ice cream.

Butterscotch Sauce

50g (2oz) butter
100g (4oz) soft brown sugar
2 tablespoons golden syrup
140ml (¼ pint) whipping cream

METHOD
1. Place butter, sugar and syrup in a double saucepan and heat gently until sugar has melted.
2. Add cream and cook, stirring constantly for 2-3 minutes. Serve warm or cold with vanilla dairy ice cream.

Green Beans with Water Chestnuts

340g (12oz) frozen green beans
1 onion, finely chopped
25g (1oz) butter
1 teaspoon lemon juice
1 clove garlic, crushed
seasoning
1 x 225g (8oz) can water chestnuts, drained and finely chopped
140ml (¼ pint) natural yogurt or soured cream

Serves 4-6   *Oven Wattage 700*

METHOD
1. Place green beans in a suitable covered dish with 6 tablespoons of salted water. Cover and cook on high for 8 minutes or until tender, stirring once.
2. Leave to stand for 3 minutes before draining off the water.
3. Combine onion and butter in a medium sized casserole dish and microwave on high for 3 minutes.
4. Add the onions, lemon juice, garlic, seasoning and water chestnuts to the beans and mix well. Cover and microwave on high for 2 minutes.
5. Stir in the yogurt or soured cream and serve hot or cold.

Fish Fillets Veronique

4 fillets white fish (450g (1lb) approx. in weight)
140ml (¼ pint) dry white wine
40g (1½ oz) butter
1 onion, finely chopped
40g (1½ oz) plain flour
140ml (¼ pint) milk
½ lemon, finely grated rind and juice
salt and black pepper
70ml (⅛ pint) double cream
100g (4oz) seedless green grapes, halved

Serves 4   *Oven Wattage 700*

METHOD
1. Half each fillet lengthwise, roll up and place in a buttered shallow dish. Pour wine into dish cover with clingfilm and cook on high for 5 minutes.
2. Place butter in a bowl and heat on high for 45 seconds. Add onion and cook on high for 1 minute. Stir in flour then gradually add milk.
3. Strain cooked fish and add liquid to sauce mixture. Cook on high for 3 minutes, stirring every minute.
4. Add lemon rind and juice to sauce. Season. Stir in cream and half the grapes then pour sauce over fish and heat on 70% power for 2 minutes. Serve garnished with remaining grapes.

Barley Vegetable Crunch

50g(2oz) butter
1 large onion, chopped
150g(6oz) pearl barley
225g(8oz) button mushrooms, washed and sliced
1 x 340g(12oz) can sweetcorn, drained
560ml(1 pint) vegetable stock
½ teaspoon paprika
½ teaspoon cinnamon
Seasoning

Topping:
100g(4oz) cheddar cheese, grated
50g(2oz) wholemeal breadcrumbs

Serves 4-6   Oven Wattage 700

METHOD
1. Melt butter in a deep casserole dish on high for 30 seconds. Add onion then cover and cook on high for 2 minutes until soft.
2. Stir in barley and cover and cook on high for 5 minutes, stirring halfway through cooking.
3. Add mushrooms, corn, stock and spices. Season.
4. Cover and cook on high for ½ hour, stirring every 10 minutes.
5. Stand covered for 10-15 minutes then transfer to a shallow ovenproof dish.
6. Mix topping ingredients together, sprinkle over dish and brown under grill.

Rice Ring with Yogurt Dressing

25g (1oz) butter
2 spring onions, sliced
1 stick celery, chopped
½ red pepper, chopped
225g (8oz) long grain rice
560ml (1 pint) vegetable stock
salt and black pepper

Dressing:
1 x 125g (5oz) carton natural yogurt
1 teaspoon fresh chives, chopped

Serves 6   Oven Wattage 700

METHOD
1. Melt butter in a large casserole dish on high for 30 seconds, add vegetables then cover and cook on high for 2 minutes.
2. Add rice and stock then cover and cook on high for 12 minutes. Leave to stand for 6 minutes until rice has absorbed all the stock. Season.
3. Press well into a wet ring mould (22cm/9" diameter) and leave to become cold. Chill for 2-3 hours.
4. Mix chives into yogurt and place in a small bowl or ramekin dish.
5. Turn ring out onto serving plate and dust with paprika pepper. Serve with bowl of yogurt dressing in centre of ring.

NOTE: For a Hot Rice Ring – reheat on the serving dish in the microwave for 4-5 minutes and serve immediately with chilled yogurt dressing.

Cheddar Fondue

1 clove garlic
140ml (¼ pint) milk
140ml (¼ pint) dry white wine
1 tablespoon cornflour
450g (1lb) cheddar cheese, grated
15g (½oz) butter
black pepper
pinch nutmeg

Serves 6   Oven Wattage 700

METHOD
1. Rub the inside of a 1.1 litre (2 pint) casserole or souffle style dish with garlic.
2. Pour the milk into the dish and heat on high for 1 minute.
3. Blend the cornflour with the cheese and add to dish. Stir in the wine then heat on high for 6 minutes, stirring every 2 minutes until the cheese has melted and mixture is thick and creamy.
4. Stir in butter, pepper and nutmeg. Serve immediately with meatballs, crisp vegetables and bread for dipping.

Minty Meatballs

70ml (⅛ pint) milk
25g (1oz) fresh white breadcrumbs
225g (8oz) lean minced beef
½ onion, finely chopped
½ teaspoon dried mint
seasoning

Oven Wattage 700

METHOD
1. Stir the breadcrumbs into the milk then leave to stand for 10 minutes.
2. Put mince in a bowl, mix in onion, mint and seasoning.
3. Add breadcrumb mixture and beat well.
4. Divide mixture into 32 equal pieces and shape into walnut-sized balls. Place in a large shallow dish (16 at a time) and cook on high for 2 minutes, turn meatballs over and cook for another 2 minutes. Serve hot or cold with cheddar fondue.

Vanilla Sponge Pudding

2 digestive biscuits, crushed
100g (4oz) butter
100g (4oz) soft brown sugar
2 eggs, beaten
½ teaspoon vanilla essence
100g (4oz) self raising flour, sieved
4 tablespoons milk

Serves 4-6   Oven Wattage 700

METHOD

1. Butter a ¾ litre (1½ pint) pudding basin and coat with biscuit crumbs.
2. Cream the butter and sugar together in a bowl until light and fluffy.
3. Gradually beat in eggs and essence alternately with the flour then stir in the milk.
4. Spoon the mixture into bowl, cover loosely with clingfilm and cook on high for 6 minutes. Stand for 5 minutes then turn out and serve with Creamy Fudge Sauce. Also delicious served with custard or cream.

Variations:
Flavour the sponge with the grated rind of a lemon or orange
Add ½ teaspoon ground ginger or cinnamon
Add 50g (2oz) sultanas or raisins

Creamy Fudge Sauce

125g (5oz) fromage frais or soured cream
100g (4oz) soft brown sugar

Oven Wattage 700

METHOD

1. Blend fromage frais or soured cream with the sugar in a pyrex jug.
2. Cook on 50% power for 1 minute then stir. Heat again for 2-3 minutes, stirring every minute until sugar has melted and sauce is thick but do not boil.
3. Serve warm with vanilla sponge pudding. Also delicious over ice cream or fruit.

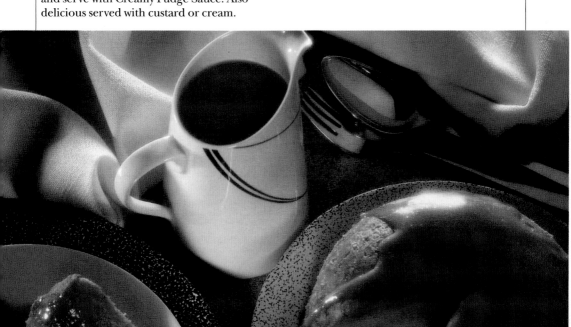

Café Crème Caramel

Caramel:

50g (2oz) caster sugar
2 tablespoons water

Egg Custard:

2 eggs
1 egg yolk
50g (2oz) caster sugar
280ml (½ pint) milk
1 dessertspoon instant coffee powder

To decorate:

140ml (¼ pint) double cream, whipped

Serves 4   Oven Wattage 700

METHOD
1. To make caramel – blend sugar and water together in a heatproof jug. Cook on high for 4-5 minutes. Check mixture every minute and as soon as caramel is golden, remove from oven and quickly coat the base of 4 ramekin dishes.
2. Heat milk in a jug on high for 3 minutes. Meanwhile lightly whisk eggs, yolk and sugar together in a bowl.
3. Stir coffee powder into hot milk then blend into egg mixture. Strain custard over caramel then place ramekins in a shallow dish and fill dish with 2 ½ cm (1") water.
4. Cook on 70% power for 10-12 minutes until custards are set. Allow to cool then chill well. Turn out onto a serving dish and decorate with cream.

Creamy Rice 'n' Raisin Pudding

50g (2oz) pudding rice
560ml (1 pint) milk
25g (1oz) soft brown sugar
50g (2oz) raisins
grated rind ½ lemon
2 tablespoons double cream

Serves 4   Oven Wattage 700

METHOD
1. Put rice, milk and sugar in a (2.8 litre/5 pint) heatproof bowl. Cover and cook on high for 5 minutes stirring after 2 minutes.
2. Stir in raisins and lemon rind and cook on 70% power for 25 minutes, stirring every 10 minutes.

3. After cooking, stand covered for 5 minutes.
4. Allow pudding to cool slightly then stir in double cream and serve hot or cold.

Black Forest Gâteau

Sponge:

125g (5oz) self raising flour	
25g (1oz) drinking chocolate powder	sieved together
1 teaspoon baking powder	
150g (6oz) butter	
150g (6oz) caster sugar	
3 eggs	
3 tablespoons milk	

Decoration:

2 tablespoons Kirsch or Brandy
3 tablespoons black cherry jam
280ml (½ pint) double cream, whipped
25g (1oz) grated chocolate

METHOD   Oven Wattage 700

1. Grease and line the base of a 20cm (8") ovenproof glass dish or round cake dish.
2. Cream butter and sugar together in a bowl.
3. Mix eggs and milk together and gradually beat into creamed mixture alternately with sieved flour.
4. Place mixture in dish and cook on high for 7-8 minutes, then stand for 5 minutes.
5. Cool on a wire tray then split sponge in half and sprinkle base of cake with a little Kirsch.
6. Spread sponge base with some whipped cream then cover with a layer of jam and place other half of sponge on top.
7. Spread top and sides with remaining cream and sprinkle on grated chocolate then finish by piping top with cream rosettes.

Variation – Chocolate Sandwich:
Fill and decorate with chocolate butter icing made with 150g (6oz) butter, 340g (12oz) icing sugar, 1 tablespoon chocolate powder and 2-3 tablespoons milk. Decorate with grated chocolate.

Cheese Gammon and Banana Rolls

Oven temperature:	180°C/350°F/No. 4
Position in oven:	centre
Time in oven:	20-30 minutes

Sauce:

25g (1oz) butter

25g (1oz) plain flour

280ml (½ pint) milk

150g (6oz) cheddar cheese, grated

seasoning

4 large bananas, peeled

4 slices gammon

Serves 4

METHOD

1. Melt butter in pan, blend in flour to make a roux.

2. Cook roux stirring for 1 minute then gradually blend in milk.

3. Return to heat, bring to the boil, stirring all the time. Cook for 2-3 minutes. Remove from heat. Season and stir in half the cheese.

4. Roll each banana up in a slice of gammon, place in an ovenproof dish, pour cheese sauce over top and sprinkle with rest of cheese. Bake until golden brown.

Vegetable Pilaff

50g (2oz) butter
1 onion, chopped
275g (10oz) frozen stir fry mixed vegetables
225g (8oz) long grain rice
4 tablespoons white wine
560ml (1 pint) chicken stock
½ teaspoon mixed spice
½ teaspoon paprika
salt and black pepper

Serves 4-6

METHOD

1. Melt 40g (1½ oz) butter in a large non-stick frying pan. Gently fry onion until soft. Add stir fry mix and cook gently for 2-3 minutes.

2. Add rice and cook, stirring occasionally for a further 3 minutes. Season and add spices.

3. Blend in wine and stock then bring to the boil.

4. Cover and simmer over low heat for 20-25 minutes until rice is tender. Stir through rest of butter and serve.

Pizza Base

225g (8oz) self raising flour
½ teaspoon salt
50g (2oz) butter
50g (2oz) cheddar cheese, grated
140ml (¼ pint) milk

METHOD

1. Sieve flour and salt into bowl then rub in butter to give a breadcrumb consistency.

2. Stir in cheese. Add milk and mix to a soft dough.

3. Turn out onto a floured board and knead lightly.

4. Roll out one 25cm (10") pizza base (or make individual bases) and place on a greased baking tray.

Party Pizza

25g (1oz) butter

1 onion, finely chopped

100g (4oz) button mushrooms, sliced

1 x 225g (8oz) can chopped tomatoes

50g (2oz) sweetcorn

½ teaspoon Italian seasoning or mixed herbs

salt and black pepper

50g (2oz) wafer thin ham

50g (2oz) cheddar cheese, grated

red or green peppers, sliced

Oven temperature:	220°C/425°F/No. 7
Position in oven:	centre
Time in oven:	25-30 minutes

Serves 4-6

METHOD

1. Fry onions and mushrooms in butter until soft then stir in tomatoes and corn.

2. Spread mixture over base and sprinkle with herbs and seasoning.

3. Arrange ham, cheese and pepper rings on top.

4. Bake in oven and serve.

Choux Pastry

50g (2oz) butter	
pinch sugar	
70ml (⅛ pint) milk	
70ml (⅛ pint) water	
65g (2½oz) plain flour	} sieved together
pinch salt	
2 eggs, beaten	

METHOD

1. Heat butter, sugar, milk and water gently in a pan until butter melts then bring to the boil.

2. Remove pan from heat and add flour. Beat in flour with a wooden spoon until mixture is smooth and leaves the sides of the pan.

3. Cool slightly then gradually add the eggs.

4. Beat well until the mixture is smooth, shiny and stands in soft peaks when spoon is lifted.

Profiterole Pyramid

1 quantity choux pastry
140ml (¼ pint) double cream
2 tablespoons Heather Cream Liqueur (optional)
1 quantity chocolate sauce (see page 79)

Oven temperature: 200°C/400°F/No. 6
Position in oven: centre
Time in oven: 20 minutes

Serves 4-6

(makes 18-20 profiteroles)

METHOD

1. Spoon the choux pastry into a large piping bag fitted with a lcm (½") plain pipe.

2. Pipe walnut size balls onto a buttered baking tray and bake until well risen and golden brown.

3. Make a hole in the bottom of each profiterole and when cool fill with whipped cream (and liqueur if used).

4. Pile profiteroles onto a serving dish and trickle some chocolate sauce over the pyramid. Serve with remaining sauce.

Genoese Sponge

50g (2oz) butter, melted and cooled	
75g (3oz) plain flour	sieved together twice
25g (1oz) cornflour	
4 large eggs	
100g (4oz) caster sugar	

Preparation of Tin
Grease a 20cm (8") loose bottomed cake tin and line with buttered greaseproof paper and dust with flour.

Oven temperature: 190°C/375°F/No. 5
Position in oven: centre
Time in oven: 30 minutes

A Genoese sponge is a whisked egg sponge mixture with the addition of butter. It is a richer mixture and needs baking slightly longer but keeps better than an egg sponge.

METHOD

1. Whisk eggs and sugar together with an electric mixer until pale and thick enough to leave a trail when whisk is lifted.

2. Fold in half the sieved flour with a metal spoon.

3. Pour in the cooled melted butter in a thin stream at the side of the bowl. Fold in the rest of the flour.

4. Pour the mixture into prepared tin and bake until well risen and firm. Cool on a wire tray.

Lemon Layer Cake

1 x 20cm (8") round Genoese sponge with finely grated rind of 1 lemon added to eggs/sugar at stage 1

125g (5oz) caster sugar

25g (1oz) cornflour

1 egg

juice of 1 lemon

280ml (½ pint) double cream

lemon jelly slices

METHOD

1. Beat sugar, cornflour and egg together then add lemon juice. Place bowl over pan of hot water, stir until thick.

2. Remove from heat and leave to become cold and thick. Whip cream and fold into lemon mixture.

3. Cut the sponge into 3 equal layers and sandwich together with some lemon cream.

4. Cover top and sides with the remaining lemon cream. Mark the cake into portions and decorate with lemon slices.

INDEX